I0416087

# The Gay Guy's Guide to Werewolves and Other Man Beasts

---

## Book 1

## Books in the Gay Guy's Guide to Werewolves Series:

### Book 1: Werewolves in History, Myths, and Folklore

Book one in the series introduces concepts related to werewolves and shapeshifting and ties that into the history, myths, and folklore of various cultures. Where possible, links between werewolfism and LGBT folks are made. She-wolves, werebears, gender-shifting, and human-animal hybrids are also explored.

### Book 2: Werewolves in Popular Culture – coming soon!

Book two will start with information on wolves, medical lycanthropy, shamanism, and werewolves as a metaphor for homosexuality. The main focus of book two will be LGBT werewolves (and other shape and gender shifters) in popular culture including movies, television shows, fiction writing, and music.

### Book 3: Modern Werewolves and Wolf Packs – coming soon!

Book three will include information on modern werewolves and how to create your own wolf pack. Otherkin, furry, and therianthrope cultures will be explored. Wolf related holidays and celebrations will be put forth, including ways to celebrate them. Wolf, werewolf, and other shapeshifting ceremonies, rituals, and spells will be included.

# The Gay Guy's Guide to Werewolves and Other Man Beasts

## Book 1: Werewolves in History, Myths, and Folklore

### Mel Mystery

Matrixwerx
2016

Copyright © 2016 by Mel Mystery

All rights reserved. This book or any portion thereof may not be reproduced without the express written permission of the publisher except for the use of short quotations for educational purposes, reviews, or to help promote this book or the information herein.

First Printing: 2015

First Edition

ISBN: 978-1-365-06031-1

Matrixwerx Photography and Web Publishing
P.O. Box 41462
Norfolk, VA 23541

www.melmystery.com

Cover Art: "The Wolf Man" by Mel Mystery

# Table of Contents

# About the Author

Mel Mystery is the host of the Discovering the Male Mysteries podcast for gay and bisexual Pagan men. Topics discussed on the show have included gay and bisexual deities, gay clone culture, mentorship, gay men who are over the traditional gay scene, gay and bi men's rites of passage, rainbows, unicorns, and gay werewolves. Mel is in the process of turning some of his show material and research into e-books – notably his continuing research into werewolves, as well as gay and bi men's rites of passage. Mel also dabbles in photography, and while most of his photography falls into the male beefcake genre, he has done some sets related to mythology and folklore and hopes to do more of these sets in the future.

Mel spent his college years in the early 1990s as an activist in his college's gay and lesbian student union. He was instrumental in making many positive changes on his campus for the LGBT cause. At one point his life was even threatened and his car was vandalized. At this time, he also served on the board of his local LGBT pride organization which organized summer and winter pride festivals. After graduating, Mel briefly canvassed for the Human Rights Campaign and also volunteered for a short time at his city's AIDS organization. Mel wrote a handful of freelance articles for his area's LGBT paper in the late 1990s. In the early 2000s, he wrote a few freelance articles for his local Pagan paper.

Mel had always felt drawn to the Pagan and New Age sections at the bookstores, and became more serious in his interest around 1999. In 2001, Mel became involved in a nearby Pagan men's group and a fraternal / revivalist Druid organization (both original groups have since dispersed). As part of these groups, Mel, along with his compatriots, was involved in planning and orchestrating rites of passage, initiations, seasonal rituals, workshops, and annual spring men's retreats at a nearby campground.

Mel considers himself an eclectic seeker who is always learning and who has much yet to learn. He has a special interest in fraternal Druidry, Norse

Paganism, classical Hellenism, and finding the threads of homosexuality, bisexuality, and phallicism in mythology and folklore. Mel also has an abnormal obsession with elves, werewolves, and brightly colored foods and drinks.

Find more at: www.melmystery.com

# Preface

I write this book from the perspective of a pagan, gay man with an interest in werewolves. The reader does not have to be pagan, gay, or male to get something from this book, but an interest in werewolves is an assumed prerequisite.

I began studying paganism around 1999 and somewhere around 2002 I had my first mystical encounter with a wolf. Little did I know it would someday become an ally and a totem. At the time, I lived in an urban neighborhood that was bordered by the Elizabeth River in Norfolk, Virginia. I lived about eight blocks from the water. I used to go walking by the river at night to clear my head. On one such night, as a full moon glistened on the river, I returned home from my walk. I was about a block from home and across the street I spied the creature. At first I thought it was a dog, but it was much larger, its snout was longer, its legs longer, and its body lithe and thin. I'd seen wolves on television and in pictures, and this was definitely one of them. A feeling of fear filled me. What if it decided to attack me? It didn't. In fact, it continued on its way not paying me any mind at all. Then it disappeared into the night. I quickened my step and returned home. Every so often I glanced back to make sure it wasn't following me. What was this wolf doing loose in the city? Did it escape from the nearby zoo? Was it someone's exotic pet? Given the full moon, could it have been a true lycanthrope? I'll likely never know the real answer. All I can say is that the experience filled me with a sense of awe and wonder, and that the experience felt mystical and supernatural somehow.

In the mid-2000s, one of the pagan men's groups I was involved in at the time adopted the wolf archetype as a kind of mascot. Many of the members were into wolves. At that point I was kind of borderline; I've always been more of a cat person than a dog person if you know what I mean. Not to mention, wolves seemed trendy in the Pagan community and I've never been one to follow the trends. At that point, I really wasn't ready to accept the wolf as a personal totem.

In the fall of 2006, our group went on a field trip to a wolf preserve a couple of hours away. The preserve held regular "howling" sessions where it would take groups of people out onto the preserve at night to listen to the wolves howl. The night we went they were pretty quiet. The ranger explained that happens sometimes. Some of the other people in our group weren't as quiet or reverent as they were supposed to be and this probably spooked the wolves. It was still a fun adventure and I did get to hear the wolves howl by purchasing a CD. The proceeds from the purchase went to the wolf reserve.

The following January, our group decided to do a werewolf ritual that we found in book at Edgar Cayce's A.R.E. center. At the time, this was supposedly the second largest occult library in the world, second only to the Vatican's archives. On the January wolf moon in 2007, we assembled at a private home on the oceanfront in Virginia Beach. There were about five of us. We made a fire on the beach and brewed up the potion and ointment mentioned in the book – among the ingredients were poppy seeds, aloe, henbane, parsley, nightshade, and camphor. Okay, so we may have substituted a few ingredients here and there. Like we used Crisco instead of the "rendered fat of a cat." One of our members donned a wolf mask and served as the gatekeeper to the circle. We danced shirtless around the fire chanting "Hail, hail, hail, great Wolf Spirit, hail! A boon we ask thee mighty shade within this circle we have made. Make us werewolves strong and bold…" and other such lines. We tried to keep it as authentic as possible, given the general lack of cat's fat and bat's blood. The experience was very surreal. To my knowledge no one actually turned into a wolf or werewolf, but then again who knows.

Over the years, wolves and werewolves have grown on me to the point that I've embraced them. Perhaps it's because of the general increase in popularity of werewolves in the popular media, or perhaps because the experience of werewolves parallels that of being gay. You discover a part of yourself that the rest of the world doesn't understand and you may even have to deal with scared villagers with torches and pitchforks – I've been there and done that and got the t-shirt. As to werewolves in the media, I've enjoyed werewolves in such movies as **Blood and Chocolate**, the **Twilight** series, **Red Riding Hood**, the **Underworld** series, and such television shows as MTV's **Teen Wolf**, Syfy's **Bitten**, the **Vampire Diaries**, and **Wolfblood**, as well as countless others that are on my list of things to watch. It doesn't hurt that many of these werewolves are sexy man beasts.

A while back in March 2014, I was in a class on Norse magick. We did an exercise to find our "fetch" – a kind of astral guide or servant attached to each person's body and soul. I was excited to discover mine was in the form of a shadowy black wolf with glowing red eyes. Its form was very metaphorical to my own nature. The wolf's outside is very subtle and obscure, but its eyes burn with a deep passion from inside. It appears aloof and even kind of threatening at the offset, but when you get to know it, it's loyal, fun, and playful like a puppy dog.

I've periodically run a group in my community called the "Wolf Pack Gathering." At first, it was only loosely related to wolves. In recent years, I've focused more on the wolf aspect and usually hold events near the full moon. Events have included werewolf themed movie nights, an occasional wolf or werewolf ceremony, fun times socializing around the fire bowl, full moon parties, and sometimes workshops related to wolf and werewolf lore.

As for this book, my intention is to give a history and mythology of werewolves with a particular focus on making connections between werewolves and homosexuality. As a gay man, my focus is on the male aspects of werewolves, but I have included several tidbits related to lesbians and transgender folks. I have also included some information on other animal transformations, particularly bears since there is an entire segment of modern gay culture that identifies with the bear. In later sections not yet written, I'll discuss other modern lycanthrope-related subcultures such as otherkin, furries, and therianthropes. I'll touch on werewolves in popular media, especially those of gay interest. Finally, for those who want to take things a step further, I'll provide information on starting your own wolf pack and some werewolf rites and observances you may want to try individually or as part of a pack.

This book is meant to be educational as well as entertaining. It is not intended as a scholarly work, though I have done my best to ensure the information is accurate. My sources include the internet, books, and personal experience - with some amount of creative license and conjecture thrown in. I will provide a bibliography for further reading at the end, but as my research has been an organic process I cannot promise that it includes every single source that influenced my writing. Internet sites are especially problematic as I've read through many of them and didn't always bookmark the pages I visited.

This book will be released in parts. There's a great deal of research involved and I juggle many priorities in my life. The first release, book 1, includes an introduction to lycanthropy and werewolfism and their place in the history, mythology, and folklore of various cultures throughout history. I've included connections to homosexuality, bisexuality, transgenderism, and general sexuality where I could. Book 2 will talk about wolves and werewolves in real life, in pop culture, and how werewolfism can often be used as a metaphor for homosexuality. Book 3 will give ideas and blue prints for creating your own wolf pack group, celebrating wolf related holidays, performing wolf rituals and ceremonies, and creating your own werewolf talismans and shapeshifting lotions.

I hope you enjoy.

Sincerely,
Mel Mystery

# Introduction

When I first set out writing this book, I expected it would be a relatively short book and that I wouldn't actually find many connections between werewolves and homosexuality in a historical context. I figured most of what I would find would be modern metaphorical connections between werewolves and homosexuality, especially in the cinema and other fiction. I didn't have a clue there was such a rich ancient history connecting werewolves and shapeshifting to homosexuality, bisexuality, transgenderism, and other forms of alternative sexualities. In some cultures, shapeshifting and homosexuality were held in high esteem. In others, they were seen as signs of deviancy and debauchery, if not pure evil.

In my research, I have found a number of underlying themes related to the connections between homosexuality and lycanthropy. Some of these themes are strong and need little justification; while others require an open mind or a stretch of the imagination. To give you an idea of what to look for, I will list those major themes here in the introduction.

## Werewolfism as a Metaphor

The connection between puberty and werewolfism is well known. Puberty is like werewolfism in that the body changes, hair starts sprouting in places where it wasn't before, and one starts having unfamiliar urges and emotions. Lesser known is the metaphor between homosexuality and werewolves. Both LGBT folks and werewolves have traditionally lived at the edges of society and they are often seen as social or sexual "deviants." Both have a dual nature merging masculine and feminine energies, as well as solar and lunar. Werewolves and LGBT folks must come to accept themselves and they might lead a closeted life. They might have to live a closeted life because villagers scared of their differences fear that they might harm or corrupt the youth. LGBT folks and werewolves might be born that way; they might have turned that way because of an experience they had; or they may have made a conscious choice.

## Gender-Variant Gods, Goddesses, and Heroes with Wolf or Werewolf Associations

A number of deities and heroes in ancient mythologies were homosexual, bisexual, or transgender. Many of these same figures, also had associations with wolves, werewolves, and shapeshifting.

## Coming of Age Rites and Warrior Initiations

Both homosexuality and shapeshifting are common in rites of passage into adulthood and in the warrior initiations in many cultures. Homosexuality and shapeshifting are often incorporated into these rituals and their associated practices.

## Many Shapeshifters Can Also Change Gender

Transgenderism is frequently associated with shapeshifting as gender-shifting is a similar trait. Sometimes they did this with the intent of luring other men into their clutches, for good or ill. Some gender-shifters even got married and / or had children. These children often inherited the ability to shapeshift or other supernatural abilities.

## Shamanic Practices Often Involved a Combination of Homosexuality, Cross-dressing, and Shapeshifting

Gender-variant individuals often fill(ed) the roles of shamans and priests. As a matter of practice, they experimented with liminal states including states between male and female and between human and animal. Many took on animal skins as a form of drag; while others took on the astral forms of animals.

## Some Werewolves Were Also Accused, Confirmed, or Strongly Implied to Be Homosexual or Bisexual

In mythological tales, some shapeshifters had confirmed or strongly implied same-sex "close friends" or known lovers. They may have exclusively had same-sex lovers and "friends" or they may have also had opposite-sex partners. These were often in cultures where some form of homosexuality or bisexuality was common, accepted, or even expected.

Later, those accused of being werewolves (such as during the Witch Trials) were often associated with homosexuality, sodomy, or other forms of social and sexual "deviancy."

## Modern LGBT Folks Can Overlay Their Own Archetypes Into Past Werewolf Stories and Myths

Myths and archetypes are timeless and are continually reinterpreted in various times and places. Whether or not past stories, myths, and folklore about shapeshifting can be historically proven to relate to homosexuality, modern folks can discover and attach their own meanings and significance to these timeless stories.

The chapters that follow will expound on these themes.

# Part 1: An Introduction to Lycanthropy and Werewolfism

# Chapter 1: An Introduction to Lycanthropy and Werewolfism

Therianthropy is the physical transformation of humans into animals through shapeshifting. In folklore and mythology, the most common form of therianthropy is lycanthropy. Lycanthropy is the transformation of humans into wolves. Other common forms of therianthropy include cynanthropy (the transformation of humans into dogs) and ailuranthropy (the transformation of humans into cats, tigers, leopards, lynx's and other felines). Other human animal transformations include humans transforming into bears, boars and pigs, foxes, hyenas, rats, rabbits and hares, birds, swans, eagles, goats, horses, cattle and bulls, seals, deer, and even crocodiles. Pretty much any animal on earth is fair game. Folklore and mythology are also filled with many animal human hybrids such as centaurs, minotaurs, mermaids, nagas, and animal headed gods such as many of the Egyptian gods. This is called theriocephaly.

The term werewolf literally means man-wolf. In some cases, the man is said to turn completely into a wolf. In others he is a combination of wolf and man. He may be a man with wolfish features or he may be an anthropomorphized wolf that has some human characteristics such as the ability to walk on two legs. Some werewolves are men wearing wolf skins. In many shamanistic traditions, the shaman doesn't physically transform into an animal. Instead he takes on the astral form of an animal or perhaps attaches his consciousness to an already existing animal. In some magickal traditions, shapeshifting is used as a mental exercise where the practitioner mentally envisions himself taking on the attributes and personality of animals, plants, and objects to gain a greater understanding of their nature or to incorporate aspects of their nature into himself. In this case, the man only changes into a wolf in his mind. The flip side to this is the delusional man who really thinks he's a wolf.

The werewolf has been called other names in other cultures. In France, he is the loup-garou. Among the Norse, he was called the varúlfur, whereas the Úlfhéðnar were Norse warriors who adopted the wolf as a totem and wore wolf skins into battle. Berserkers were similar warriors who wore bear skins. The Celts had comparable wolf warriors known as the Bleiden and the Faelad. In Greece, they were called lycanthropos, where "lycan" means "wolf" and "anthropos" means "man." In Rome, they were called versapellis meaning "turn coat." Icelandic werewolves are known as Kvelv-Ulf and other Scandinavian countries such as Denmark, Norway, and Sweden called their werewolves Varulv. Werewolves are known as Varcolac, Verfarkas, Vourdalak, and Vovkulaka in Romania, Hungary, Russia, and Ukrainia, respectively. Spanish werewolves are known as Hombre Lobo and Italian werewolves are known as Lupo Manero. Native Americans referred to their shapeshifters as skinwalkers.

There are many reasons one might become a werewolf or other were-creature. Many of these are similar to how one might become homosexual, bisexual, or transgendered. Firstly, one might simply be born that way. Perhaps he's the offspring of other shapeshifters, of an animal-human coupling, the coupling between a human and a deity in animal form, or a human and some other supernatural creature. One can become a werewolf by being bitten (and sometimes scratched) by a werewolf. For LGBT folks bitten could be a metaphor for sexual intercourse, as someone repressing their own desires might "become" gay or bisexual after having a liberating homosexual experience. One might become a werewolf on purpose through some spell, ritual, or enchantment. Magical shapeshifting was a common theme in many cultures and spells and rituals to become a werewolf exist in these cultures. In some cases, one becomes a werewolf by giving in to his carnal addictions – whether bloodlust, sexual lust, or some other "immoral" compulsion. It could be that the transformation into animal or beast is a reflection of one's true nature which is being revealed through the transformation. It could also be that an animal spirit or soul is trapped in the body of a human, perhaps through reincarnation. This is similar to the concept among the transgendered about being a woman trapped in a man's body or being a man trapped in a woman's body. Another way one might become a werewolf is to be turned through the sorcery or magical powers of others including being turned by deities. Often this is seen in the form of someone being cursed by a magician or punished by a god or goddess for one's misdeeds.

More obscure ways to become a werewolf include eating a wolf's brain, drinking water out of a wolf's paw print, or by drinking from a stream where three or more wolves have been seen to drink. Those born on the winter solstice, Christmas Eve, or Christmas Day are also reputed as likely to become werewolves. For Christians, being born on Christ's birthday[1] might be deemed an insult to their savior and reason enough to be cursed with lycanthropy. For Pagans, the dark time of the winter solstice and deep of winter is believed to attract dark and malevolent creatures. The idea is that the solstices open up portals to other planes of existence. These portals open the way for outside forces to enter into our world.

The benefits of becoming a werewolf are complex, especially since becoming a werewolf also has its downsides. Traditionally people aspired to become werewolves and other shapeshifters to gain the powers and knowledge of the animal; to scare enemies in battle; or to allow them to commit crimes, including murder, in wolf form thereby concealing their true identities. Modern folks might want to become a werewolf to gain strength, for the heightened senses, or to benefit from an accelerated healing process. It should be noted that accelerated werewolf healing is a modern invention. In antiquity accelerated

---

[1] Alleged birthday. Many scholars believe that Christ was born in the spring. The winter solstice was adopted as Christ's birthday by early Christians to coincide with pre-Christian winter solstice festivals and to associate Christ with Pagan gods said to be born on the winter solstice. In doing so, early Christians hoped to capitalize on the popularity of these festivals and better convert the heathen masses to Christianity.

werewolf healing powers did not exist. In fact, werewolves were often identified in part due to cuts and lashes they were believed to acquire as a werewolf while crawling through the underbrush and other injuries received while in wolf form. Sometimes as a wolf they were shot, maimed, or they may have lost a limb or other extremity. When they reverted to human form their injuries were taken as proof that they were the injured werewolves. Downsides to being a werewolf include excessive body hair, sometimes painful transformations, uncontrollable bloodlust, and pursuit by angry villagers and werewolf hunters.

Supposedly there a ways to identify werewolves. Things to look out for include thick unibrows, low-set ears, curved fingernails, long middle fingers[2], and hairy palms, though the last is also an alleged sign of excessive masturbation. The pentagram symbol might appear in the palms or other areas of the body. The eyes can also be a sign of werewolfism in both human and wolf form. Werewolves are said to keep their human eyes in wolf form, and in human form their eyes are distinctive, wild, and enthralling.

Not all werewolves want to be werewolves. Even among those who are comfortable with their own werewolf nature, there are often family, friends, and other busy bodies overly concerned with their nocturnal habits. A lot of werewolves decide to stay in the closet for this reason. Others feel forced to denounce their werewolfism on religious and "moral" grounds. The same can be said for many LGBT folks.

Some alleged cures for werewolfism make modern ex-gay Ministries and conversion therapy seem tame by comparison - though some of these probably mirror extreme "cures" for homosexuality from less enlightened times. The Greeks and Romans believed that lycanthropy could be cured through exhaustion. If you subjected the werewolf to long periods of physical activity this might actually cure him too. Many alleged werewolves claimed to feel weak and debilitated after their shapeshifting experiences so the Greeks and Romans figured exhaustion was the cure. Sicilian and Arabic beliefs hold that a werewolf can be cured by hitting it on the forehead or scalp with a knife. Piercing the werewolf's hands with nails was also said to do the trick. One German belief states that a werewolf could be cured by addressing it three times by its Christian name. Converting to Christianity was also believed to cure werewolves. Making devotions to St. Hubert was believed to be particularly useful for curing werewolfism and for protecting oneself from werewolves. A Danish belief concludes that merely scolding the werewolf will cure it.[3] In medieval Europe, a werewolf might be cured by wolfsbane, by exorcism, or through surgery. Many of these cures proved fatal for their patients. Other cures for werewolfism include the werewolf killing the one who turned him, and possibly eating his or

---

[2] There is a modern theory that sexual orientation can be determined by relative finger lengths. Some studies suggest that men with longer index fingers than ring fingers are more likely to be gay, whereas the inverse is suggested for women.

[3] Perhaps scolding the werewolf with a rolled up newspaper. "Bad wolf." Thank you Rose Tyler.

her heart. The ultimate cure for werewolfism is death which could be effected with a silver bullet, silver in general, or decapitation. Silver and silver bullets are traditional ways to kill a variety of supernatural creatures and the werewolf's vulnerability to silver dates back at least as far as the legend of the Beast of Gévaudan from 18th century France. The gigantic wolf in this story was killed by Jean Chastel using silver bullets.

# Part 2: Wolves, Werewolves, and Shapeshifting in History, Mythology, and Folklore

# Chapter 2: Greek Lycanthropes

## Overview of Greek Werewolves

A werewolf becomes a werewolf because he is cursed by the gods, or through certain rituals and initiations.

Werewolves could be cured by waiting for the curse to end, by abstaining from human flesh for a specified time, or though exhaustion since some werewolves were believed to revert to human form once they got tired.

The bodies of dead werewolves should be destroyed or they might come back as vrykolakas – a type of undead vampire creature that scavenges battlefields for the blood of dead warriors, causes disease, and goes door to door looking for victims.

Greek mythology is full of human animal hybrids such as satyrs, centaurs, the Minotaur, and so on. These will be discussed in a later chapter.

## Background on Ancient Greek Homosexuality

The ancient Greeks were well-known for their open attitudes toward homosexuality. Many Greek gods and goddesses were homosexual, bisexual, and even transgender. Greek art including sculptures and vase paintings venerate the male form and homosexual relations. Greek philosophers such as Plato even suggest that homosexuality is a higher form of love than heterosexuality. Pederastic initiatory mentorship relationships between older males, known as erastes, and adolescent males, known as eromenos, were culturally accepted. Homosexuality was common in the Greek military and troops of male lovers, such as the Sacred Band of Thebes, were considered superior warriors because they would protect their lovers and fight valiantly to uphold the respect and honor of those lovers. Lesbian relationships in ancient Greece are less well documented, but not unheard of. The Greek poetess Sappho on the island of Lesbos wrote many love poems for other women and girls.

## The Neuri

The Greek historian Herodotus wrote in Book Four of his **Histories** about a Scythian tribe of sorcerers, possibly shamans, who transformed into wolves for a few days each year, and then turned back into humans. This tribe was called the Neuri. Later accounts of this tribe had the Neuri transforming every full moon. According to Herodotus, the Neuri were driven from their homeland by serpents. He does not go into any additional detail about the wolf transformations or beliefs of these people.

## King Lycaon

In one myth from ancient Greece, King Lycaon of Arcadia, served a meal to the Greek God Zeus made from the human flesh of his son Nyctimus to test if Zeus was really a God. As punishment for this, Zeus resurrected Nyctimus and transformed Lycaon into a wolf. Lycaon's name is where the term Lycanthropy comes from. There may also be a hidden homosexual element to this story. In many Greek myths, resurrection is used as a metaphor for homosexual initiation. In a similar story, King Tantalus kills his son Pelops and tries to feed him to the gods. The gods resurrect Pelops who is then taken as a lover by Poseidon. It has been suggested by some sources that Lycaon's resurrected son may have been taken as a lover by Zeus.[1]

## Festival and Rites of Lykaia

The ancient Greek festival of Lykaia took place each spring in the mountains of Arcadia on Mount Lykaion which means "Wolf Mountain." The festival took place at the altar of Zeus and Zeus was invoked by the epithet Lykaios or "Wolf Zeus." In addition to the annual festival and athletic games every four years, a secret rite of passage took place involving the epheboi (adolescent males). The ritual took place at night and focused on the threat of cannibalism and the possibility of the youths turning into werewolves. The ritual involved human sacrifice and the feasting on human flesh.[2] Those who partook of the human flesh were said to become a wolf for nine years and could only become human again if they avoided eating human flesh within that time frame. The ritual paralleled the story of King Lycaon which was the founding myth of the region.

In one story related to this rite, the Arcadian boxer, Damarchus, who won the Olympics around 400 BC, was said to have been transformed into a wolf for nine years after making a sacrifice to Zeus on Mount Lykaion.

In similar ritual, which is likely a later evolution of the Lykaian rite of passage, an Arcadian youth removes his clothes, swims across a marsh, and becomes a wolf and lives among the wolves for nine years. If after nine years, if he's not tasted human flesh he can return across the lake, put on his clothes, and resume human form.

---

[1] "A Brief History of Gay Werewolves: Part 1, the Ancient World", Queer Gods for Queer Men Blog, http://queergodsforqueermen.blogspot.com/2011/10/brief-history-of-gay-werewolves-part-1.html

[2] This was probably symbolic or metaphoric rather than actual cannibalism. Archaeologists have only found animal remains and no human remains at the site these rituals took place.

## People of Mount Parnassus

Another myth tells of a people associated with Mount Parnassus. These people worshiped wolves. Two differing origin stories exist for these people. In one, they were said to come from a place called Lykoreia, translated as "wolf mountain." In the other story, torrential rains flooded their original homeland, and they were said to have been lead to safety by listening to the howling wolves upon the mountain.

## Greek Deities Associated with Wolves

**Zeus** is the Greek god of the sky and thunder. He is the ruler of the Greek pantheon and is said to be the father of gods and men. Zeus is mainly known for his numerous relationships with women, much to the dismay of his wife, Hera. He had at least one male lover, Ganymede, whom Zeus (while in the form of an eagle) abducted to be the cupbearer of the gods. Zeus Lykaios, a wolf aspect of Zeus, was worshiped by the people of Mount Lykaion and honored in their festival of Lykaia.

**Charon,** the Greek ferryman who carries the souls of the dead across the rivers Styx and Acheron, is said to wear wolf ears.

**Leto** is a primal goddess associated with motherhood and protecting the young. She is daughter of the Sun and Moon Titans. She is the mother of Apollo and Artemis. Leto is sometimes known to roam in the form of a she-wolf. After the birth of Apollo and Artemis, she was said to have been guided by wolves to the River Xanthos in Lykia.

**Apollo** is a Greek god with many talents. Among other things, he is associated with music, poetry, and the arts; prophecy; medicine and healing; shepherds and flocks; and the sun. Apollo had both male and female lovers. His male lovers included Hyacinth, Cyparissus, Admetus, Atymnius, Branchus, Carnus, Clarus, Hppolytus of Sicyon, Hymenaios, Iapis, Leucates, Phorbas, and Potnieus. A number of Apollo's relationships ended tragically. Wolves are sacred to Apollo, and Apollo Lycaeus is an aspect of this god in wolf form. The Lyceum, an ancient Greek gymnasium, is dedicated to Apollo Lycaeus.

**Artemis** is the Greek goddess of hunting, wild animals, wild places, chastity, and childbirth. As with her mother and brother, Artemis is associated with wolves. Artemis is considered a "virgin" goddess in the sense that she did not have sexual relations with men. She is associated with friendship among women, and she is considered a goddess of all women. As a huntress, she refused to follow traditional gender roles. Her female lovers included: Atalanta, Britomartis, Cyrene, Anticleia, Syrinx, Taygete, Zabeta, Callisto, and Amethyst.

**Hekate** is the Greek Goddess of the night, crossroads, magic, and the Underworld. Hecate is associated with dogs and wolves. She is sometimes depicted with three faces looking into the past, present, and future. Often one or more of these faces is that of an animal including that of a dog or wolf. Other animal faces include serpents and horses. In the magical papyri of ancient Egypt she is called the "Bitch" and the "She-Wolf." Her presence is indicated by the barking of dogs. Hecate presides over a number of poisonous plants including wolfsbane. Hecate is said to have created this plant out of the foam from the mouth of Cerberus, the three-headed dog of the Underworld in Greek myth.

# Chapter 3: Roman Versipellis

## Overview of Roman Werewolves

Romans called their werewolves "versipellis" meaning "turn skin."

There is significant overlap between Greek and Roman werewolf beliefs and mythology.

The typical reasons for becoming a werewolf were either from being cursed, or through sorcery.

Wolves held a sacred and totemic place in Roman culture, particularly in Rome's founding myth.

Lupa, meaning "she-wolf," was a Roman slang term for prostitutes.

## Romulus and Remus

The mythical founders of Rome, Romulus and Remus, were said to have been raised by a she-wolf. King Numitor of Alba Longa was deposed in a coupe by his brother, Amulius, who seized the city and killed all of Numitor's male heirs. Numitor's daughter Rhea conceived the twins Romulus and Remus who were fathered by either the god Mars or in some stories the demigod Heracles. As rightful heirs in line for execution, the twins were abandoned as newborns on the banks of the Tiber River. Protected by the river deity, Tiberinus, the cradle containing the twins was carried downstream by the flooding river. A female wolf, known as Lupa, found them and suckled them, until they were later found by a shepherd and his wife who raised them to adulthood. Eventually they discovered their true origins, restored King Numitor to his throne, and set out to found their own city. In the process, they had a disagreement and Remus was killed. Romulus then founded his city and called it Rome. There are some[3] who speculate that this story is actually a metaphor for homosexual initiation into a cult of Mars. Wolves are sacred to Mars because of their hunting and warrior prowess. The she-wolf in the initiation may have been a man wearing wolf skins and the suckling may have been oral intercourse. In many tribal cultures, semen was likened to milk and was believed to have magical and life-giving powers.

---

[3] Notably the historian David Greenberg, author of the book **The Construction of Homosexuality**.

Semen was also believed to pass on a warrior's manly virtue and vitality[4]. After the initiation, the young men would take on wolf names and wear wolf skins.

## Ovid's Metamorphoses

Ovid's epic poem *"Metamorphoses"* features a variety of transformations, including changes into animals, constellations, and inanimate objects; sex changes; and color changes. Humans and an occasional nymph, are transformed into animals, birds, insects, spiders, swans, owls, plants and flowers, stones, nymphs, monsters, and even clouds and constellations. Additionally, a few animals are turned to humans. In some cases, humans were even deified as gods.

Some of these stories are from Greek mythology and have already been mentioned in the last chapter, such as the account King Lycaon and the Arcadian Rites and Festival of Lykaia. Often, the human was turned into an animal as punishment from a god or goddess. For example, Actaeon was turned into a stag for seeing the goddess Diana naked. Canen's husband was turned into a woodpecker by Circe, because he scorned Circe's love. Hippomenes and Atalante were turned into lions by the goddess Cybele for having sex in her temple. In some cases, humans were turned into plants, constellations, or gods to immortalize them for their heroism or because they were the deceased lover of a god.

Gender transformation also takes place in *Metamorphoses*. Ovid mentions a woman named Caneis who was transformed by Neptunus into the invulnerable male hero, Caeneus. In another instance, he tells the story of Hermaphroditis. Hermaphroditis is born the handsome son of Venus and Mercury. At the age of 15 he encounters the nymph Salmacis in her pool. She tries to seduce him, but he rejects her. Later he returns to her pool and thinking she is gone he undresses and enters the pool. Salmacis who was hiding nearby jumps in, tackles him, and wraps herself around him. She prays to the gods that they should never be parted. The gods grant her wish by fusing Hermaphrodotis and Salmacis into one androgynous being with the qualities and attributes of both sexes. In some stories, Hermaphrodotis is not an androgynous being, but a man who can transform into a woman. Ovid also mentions gender transformation taking place among hyenas. This gender transformation was believed by early naturalists to be a common occurrence.

---

[4] Similar adolescent homosexual initiations were recorded in Melenasia. The semen from an older man is believed to impart masculine vitality and life force to the male adolescent. The locals believed that both oral and anal homosexual intercourse and instilment of semen into the youth is necessary for his growth into manhood.

## Virgil's Eclogue

Virgil's **Eclogue VIII: Damon and Alphesiboeus Compete** mentions a powerful sorcerer who turns himself into a werewolf. Alphesiboeus is performing a love spell to bring her the love of Daphnis and she mentions she got her magickal ingredients from Moeris who could change into a wolf, summon ghosts, and magickally transport whole fields of corn.

> *Moeris himself gave me these herbs and poisons*
> *gathered from Pontus (many grow there in Pontus),*
> *I've often seen Moeris, with these, change to a wolf and hide*
> *in the woods, often call ghosts from the depths of the grave,*
> *and draw sown corn into other men's fields.*

## Pliny the Elder

In his **Natural History, Book VIII, Chapter XXII**, Pliny the Elder skeptically recounts the Greek tales about the Arcadians turning into wolves. In the same passage, Pliny mentions a special hair on the tail of the wolf that if plucked from a live wolf could be used in love potions. Of course, the wolf sheds this hair if captured thus rendering it useless.

In **Natural History, Book VII, Chapter II**, Pliny recounts a story by the Greek physician and historian Ctesias about the Cynocephali - an Indian or Ethiopian tribe of dog-headed people who lived in the mountains. These people communicated by barking, lived in caves, used weapons, and wore animal skins. Some sources believe that the cynocephali were actually baboons.

## The Satyricon

The Roman prose work, the **Satyricon**, is believed to have been written by a Roman courtier named Gaius Petronius Arbiter around the year 60 C.E. In chapters 61-62 of the novel, at a banquet a character named Niceros recounts his own eyewitness account of a houseguest turning into a werewolf. On the night of a full moon, Niceros and his guest (who was also a soldier) go on an errand. They stop in a cemetery and Niceros is surprised to see his guest strip out of all his clothes and pee in a circle around them. The clothes turn to stone and the soldier transforms into a wolf, howls, and runs off into the night.

When Niceros returns home, his wife tells of a wolf that attacked their sheep and how one of their servants ran a spear through the wolf's neck. The next morning Niceros rushes back to the spot where the soldier left his clothes only to find a puddle of blood. When he returns home a second time, the soldier is there and a doctor is treating a neck wound.

## Lupercalia

Lupercalia was celebrated in ancient Rome from February 13-15 to celebrate the anniversary of the founding of the temple of the Roman god Lupercus on February 15. Lupercus is the Roman faun god and a god of shepherds who is sometimes identified as the Roman god Faunus. He is equivalent to the Greek god Pan. The celebration also honored the she-wolf, Lupa, who was said to suckle the Roman founders, Romulus and Remus. Lupercalia is a fertility and purification rite, and may be a predecessor to the modern Valentine's Day which is observed on February 14. The celebration features wolves and naked men running through the streets flogging people with goat skins.

The festival rites were conducted by the Luperci, meaning "brothers of the wolf." These were priests of Faunus. The festival began with the sacrificing of two male goats and a dog followed by a sacrificial feast. Salt meal cakes prepared by the Vestal Virgins would be burnt as an offering. The Luperci would then cut thongs from the animals, dress scantily in the goat skins (if wearing anything at all), and run around whipping people in the crowd with the thongs. It was believed that women hit with the thongs would be ensured fertility and that they would have easier childbirths, so girls and young women would line up much like they do today to catch bouquets at a wedding. Participants were also believed to receive purification from curses and bad luck.

According to Ovid, the reason Lupercalia involves male nudity is because of a Greek myth involving Heracles, the queen Omphale, and the god Pan who is the Greek equivalent to the Roman god Faunus. Pan lusted after Omphale and snuck into the tent where she and Heracles were sleeping. Heracles and Omphale had engaged in cross-dressing wearing each other's clothes, so Pan found a big surprise when he reached under "Omphale's" dress to rape her. He had grabbed Heracles' manhood instead. Heracles kicked him out of the tent and Pan headed for the hills. After that, Pan insisted his followers should worship and celebrate in the nude so he wouldn't be surprised this way again.

## Roman Deities Associated with Wolves

**Mars** is the Roman god of war and guardian of agriculture. He rules over masculine virility and masculine aggression. Wolves were sacred to Mars. Some believe that the tale of Romulus and Remus was part of a homosexual initiation into the cult of Mars.

**Lupercus** is the Roman faun god and god of shepherds. He is a protector of the flocks against wolves. He is also associated with the Roman god Faunus and the Greek god Pan.

**Luperca** is the Roman wolf-goddess and wife of Lupercus. She is sometimes depicted in wolf form and is said to protect sheep from wolves. Some stories claim that she was the she-wolf, Lupa, that nursed Romulus and Remus. She is also known as Acca Larentia.

**Diana**, is the Roman Goddess of the Hunt, the Moon, childbirth, women, and wild animals. She is the Roman equivalent of the Greek Artemis. She is a virgin goddess who swore never to marry. Diana is associated with wolves and other wild animals.

# Chapter 4: Egyptian Wolf Headed Gods

## Overview of Egyptian Werewolves

Egyptian gods and goddesses are frequently depicted with the bodies of humans and the heads of animals, including wolves and jackals.

Wolves and jackals are strongly associated with cemeteries and the dead as they are scavengers that were likely to uncover and eat human bodies in such places. For this reason wolf and Jackal-headed gods were related to the dead and the afterlife.

The Egyptian jackal, also known as the African wolf and wolf jackal, is actually a sub-species of the gray wolf.

One myth depicts heroic wolves who are granted human forms by the god Osiris.

## Lycopolis

The Egyptian city of Asyut, also known as Lycopolis, in Upper Egypt was said to have been protected from an invading army by wolves sometime around 3100 BCE. Lycopolis is Greek for "wolf city." These wolves assisted Osiris in defending the city, and while many wolves died in the battle, the invaders were eventually defeated. For their bravery and sacrifice, Osiris renamed the city Lycopolis and had the bodies of the fallen wolves mummified and interned beneath the city so that these wolves could be resurrected in the underworld. For the wolves still living after this battle, Osiris gave them a human form in addition to their wolf form and granted them the ability to change between these forms. Archeologists have actually uncovered mummified wolves in excavated chambers of the ancient city.

## Egyptian Deities Associated with Wolves

**Anubis** is the Egyptian, jackal-headed god, who is protector of the dead and associated with embalming, mummification, and the afterlife. The Egyptian Book of the Dead shows Anubis weighing the heart of the dead to determine whether the deceased is worthy to enter the Egyptian underworld, known as Duat. The deceased one's heart is weighed against an ostrich feather representing Maat or truth. The heart must weigh less than the feather for the soul to enter the afterlife. If not, the deceased one's soul will be fed to a demon called Ammit. The Greeks and Romans sometimes associated the Egyptian Anubis with the star Sirius and with the three-headed hellhound Cerberus,

Anubis' symbols include the flail and the fetish (a stuffed, headless animal skin tied to a pole used in ancient Egyptian funeral rites).

**Duamutef** is one of the Four Sons of Horus, a group of Egyptian gods personifying the four canopic jars that contained the organs of mummified bodies. Duamutef is portrayed as a mummified body with the head of a wolf, jackal, or sometimes a falcon. His name means "he who worships his mother." His mother is the goddess Isis and his father is Horus and /or Osiris depending on the story. Duamutef is entrusted to protect the stomach organ. He in turn is protected by the goddess Neith.

**Hermanubis** is a later variation of Anubis who is merged with the Greek god Hermes. Hermanubis was worshiped in Greece and Rome as late as the 2nd century AD, and also appears in writings on alchemy and hermeticism in the European Middle Ages and Renaissance. His cult was centered in the Egyptian city of Cynopolis, meaning "city of dogs" in Greek.

**Osiris,** was an Egyptian god of the afterlife, underworld, the dead, and rebirth who was worshipped in wolf-form in the city of Lycopolis. In another myth related to Osiris, he was also a phallic god associated with the annual flooding of the Nile. In this myth, he was killed by his brother Set who wanted his throne. Set killed him and cut him into pieces. The Goddess Isis collected and rejoined the fragmented pieces but his phallus was missing. Isis shaped a phallus of gold for him and brought him back to life just long enough for them to have sex and for her to conceive Horus. Osiris' son Horus is sometimes represented as being in a homosexual relationship with the Egyptian god, Set. Set is even said to have given birth to Horus' child as a result of oral intercourse.

**Wepwawet** is the wolf headed, Egyptian god of warfare and hunting. Sometimes he is depicted as a wolf or jackal without a human body. Wepwawet means "Opener of the Ways." Other variations of his name include Upuaut, Wep-wawet, Wepawet, and Ophois. Similar to Anubis, and because of his associations with war and death, Wepwawet is sometimes given the role of a psychopomp (a guide for the souls of the dead). Wepwawet is said to open the ways for the dead to and through Duat, the Egyptian afterlife. The mace and hunting arrows are his symbols.

# Chapter 5: Celtic Shapeshifters

The theme of shapeshifting is found prominently in Celtic myth. Those who shapeshift transform or are transformed into any number of animals, birds, grains, and other objects. Because this book is about werewolves, I will mainly focus on those transformations related to wolves. However a few non-wolf shapeshifting stories will be shared here for an overall context of shapeshifting in Celtic folklore and mythology.

## Overview of Celtic Werewolves

Shapeshifting is a common topic in Celtic mythology. It was frequently used as a means of protection, survival, punishment, or a means to facilitate rebirth.

Transformation into all manner of animals and plants may take place as a result of personal magical abilities or as the result of a curse.

The Irish word for wolf is "Mac Tire" which means "son of the countryside."

Irish werewolves are called faoladh, faelad, and conroicht. They are often seen as guardians, protectors of children, and guides to the lost.

Scottish wolf headed men are known as wulver. They are benevolent toward mankind.

Ireland was once full of wolves and the Irish wolfhound was specifically bred to hunt down wolves.

In Celtic belief, the wolf is said to rule over the winter season. The month of February was called "Faoilleach," and was considered the month of the wolf.

## Reasons for Shapeshifting

Reasons for shapeshifting include punishment, protection, survival, and to facilitate rebirth. It is often through these transformations that individuals were able to gain knowledge from living as animals, to better appreciate and gain a closer affinity with nature, and to receive knowledge from otherworld beings.

## Fith-Fath

In Highland Scottish folklore there is a specific spell used for shapeshifting. This type of spell is known as fith-fath[5]. It is translated as "deer aspect" and the spell was most frequently chanted in verse. This type of spell was often used to effect a form of invisibility or camouflage by transforming a person into an animal or other form so they could walk unseen. Frequently this was used by hunters so they could get closer to their prey and also as a method to hide their slain prey from anyone who might take it. Sometimes this type of spell was used to transform objects from one form to another.

## Faoladh

Faoladh is the Irish term for werewolves. These shapeshifters are believed to be hereditary werewolves rather than becoming a werewolf through other means. They are benevolent toward humans and often serve as guardians and protectors of children, the wounded, and the lost. The Faoladh are able to speak while in wolf form. They still maintain a predatory nature, but they attack sheep, cattle, and other livestock rather than humans. If they are surprised or attacked, they revert back to human form but often show signs of their transformation such as wounds from when they were wolves or bloodstains if they attacked livestock. Another variation of their transformation has the Faoladh sending out their spirit to possess an actual wolf while their human body remains in a protected space. If their human body is moved while their soul possesses a wolf, it is said that they will not be able to locate their body and thus will not be able to return to it.

## Conroicht

There is a tale in Ireland of the people of Ossory. These people were documented by Giraldus Cambrenis in the year 1185. According to the legend, chosen pairs of male and female would transform and live as wolves for seven years. At the end of that time they would be replaced by another couple. As wolves, they would feed on livestock and help children and adults who were lost in the woods or who were wounded. Despite this being a pre-Christian legend, later Christian writers attributed the transformations to a curse from either St. Natalia or St. Patrick.

---

[5] Pronounced fee-faw.

## Laignach Faelad

The Laignach Faelad are mentioned in a 16th century Celtic text known as the **Coir Anmann: A Late Middle Irish Treatise On Personal Names**. Laignech was a man in Ossory who used to shift into Faelad, or wolf form. His descendants inherited his shapeshifting ability and could shapeshift at will. They were known as the Laignach Faelad after their ancestor. They would go about in wolf form and, like wolves, they would kill the herds.

These seem to be different than the **C**onroicht who also inhabited Ossory, though they may have been related and there seems to be some overlap in their legends. The Conroicht were said to shapeshift in male-female pairs for seven year periods, rather than transforming at will.

The Faelad are also known as the "Wolf Men of Tipperary." Some accounts suggest they were brutal wolf warriors dressed in wolf skins and that they were often recruited as mercenaries to fight for any king willing to pay their price. It is said that they asked for the flesh of newborns which they would devour. The Laignach Faelad are said to have been devoted to the god Crom Cruach ("the Bowed God of the Mounds") who is alleged to have been a terrible and bloodthirsty deity. [6]

## Wulver

In Scotland, a benevolent creature called the "wulver" has the body of a man and the head of a wolf. Wulver's lived in caves and were fond of fishing. They would catch fish off the coasts, in the rivers, and in the lochs. Sometimes they would leave fish in windowsills as gifts for the local people.

---

[6] I am somewhat skeptical of the stories of child sacrifice to the Laignach Faelad or to Crom Cruach because the prevalent stories are Christianized stories seemingly told to discredit the pre-existing Pagan religions of the time (and to praise the works of Christian saints such as Patrick). Unfortunately, I've been unable verify much in terms of source materials that mention the Laignach Faelad or the Crom Cruach and a full investigation is beyond the scope of this book. Crom Cruach is mentioned in the Coir Anmann, the Books of Leinster, of Ballymote, of Lecan, and in a document titled the Rennes MS, all of which seem to have been written after Ireland was Christianized. Most likely Crom Cruach was a dying god of the harvest. It was common in many ancient agricultural cultures to burn corn stacks at the end of the fall harvest and to sacrifice old and sickly livestock that would not likely make it through the winter. Crom Cruach's associations with wolves and werewolves may have been due to the approaching winter season as wolves were believed to rule over the winter months. Some sources suggest that Crom Cruach was a chief god and a popular god who could have been the Celtic version of Zeus, Hermes, or Apollo. Since werewolves are often associated with cannibalism, I won't discount the allegations of eating or sacrificing firstborn babies completely, but whether this was actual cannibalism or some kind of mock, symbolic cannibalism related to the harvest is up for debate.

## The Story of Taliesin

One of the best known stories of shapeshifting is the Welsh story of Taliesin as told in the **Mabinogion**. In the story, a boy named Gwion Bach tends the Cauldron of Wisdom and Inspiration for a witch named Ceridwen. The cauldron must be kept boiling for a year and a day. At that time the first three drops would impart universal knowledge to any who drank them, and the rest of the concoction would be deadly poison. Ceridwen wants the drops for her ugly son in the hopes of making him into so great a bard that no one would mind his ugliness. On the last day when the liquid was ready, three drops flew out of the cauldron onto Gwion's thumb as he was stirring. Instinctively he put his thumb into his mouth to stop the burning and was imparted ultimate knowledge and great magical powers. Ceridwen became furious and began to chase him. With his new magic, Gwion transformed himself into various animal shapes to escape the wrath of Ceridwen. Gwion transformed himself into a hare, a fish, a bird and finally a grain of wheat. Ceridwen in an attempt to catch him also transformed herself. She became a greyhound, an otter, a falcon and a hen. In the shape of a hen, she finally caught Gwion, who was at this stage a grain of wheat, she swallowed Gwion and in so doing became pregnant and eventually she gave birth to Taliesin. Ceridwen had planned to kill the child once he was born, but she was unable to do so. Instead she placed him in a basket and threw him into a lake. He was found by Elphin, who was fishing, and he became Elphin's adopted son. The reborn Gwion was named Taliesin, meaning "radiant brow" because his forehead was so white. Taliesin tells Elphin his tale including his many transformations; among these are a "wolf cub" and a "wolf in the wilderness."

## Gwydyon and Gilvaethwy

In another story of the **Mabinogion**, titled "The Maiden Under My Feet", there was a powerful sorcerer named Math who was the son of Mathonwy. He liked to rest his feet in the lap of a virgin maiden named Goewin. Math had two nephews – Gwydyon and Gilvaethwy – who were the sons of his sister Don. The two brothers were Math's advisors and helped him run the kingdom. Gilvaethwy fell in love with Goewin, but knew his uncle Math would not approve. Gwydyon devised a plan to help his brother by forcing Math's kingdom into a war. With Math leading his army, Gilvaethwy was free to pursue Goewin and he raped her.

Math eventually returned from the war to find Goewin no longer a virgin. Math punished Gilvaethwy by transforming him into a hind and his brother Gwydyon into a stag. Math sent the two into the forest to mate and to return in a year with their young. The following year, the brothers returned with a young fawn. Math transformed the fawn to human form and named the son, Hyddwn.

Math then transformed Gilvaethwy into a wild boar and Gwydyon into a wild sow. Again he sent them to the forest to mate and to return in a year with their young. The brothers returned a year later with a young pig. Math transformed the pig into a boy and named the boy, Hchdwn.

Then Math turned Gwydyon into a wolf and Gilvaethwy into a she-wolf and sent them to mate and return with their young. A year later they returned with a wolf pup. Math named him Bleiddwn and transformed him into a boy. Finally, Math felt the brothers had been punished enough and turned them back to human form.

## Airitech

In Irish mythology, Airitech was a mysterious monster of the Otherworld. His three daughters were werewolves who could transform at will or at the bidding of their father. They were eventually killed by a heroic bard named Cas Corach. The hero hypnotized the werewolves with beautiful music from his harp and then killed them.

## Cormac mac Airt

Cormac mac Airt was a High King of Ireland in Irish legend, and he may have even existed in reality. He was supposed to be a good, wise, fair, and generous king. Most of the stories of the Fenian Cycle are set during his reign. Cormac was the son of King Art mac Cuinn and his mother was named Achtan. Achtan had a dream that foretold of Art's death, but not before a son was conceived by the couple. Not long after that Achtan became pregnant and Art was killed in battle by his nephew Lugaid mac Con who became the new king. Achtan fled seeking Art's stepfather, Fiachrae Cassán. On the journey, Achtan went into labor and gave birth to Cormac in the forest. While Achtan and her nurse slept, Cormac was carried off, suckled, and raised by a she-wolf with her cubs. Some time passed and eventually a hunter found the boy and returned him to his mother.

In adulthood, Cormac regained his throne from Lugaid and became one of the most celebrated kings in Celtic mythology. It was said that Cormac was extremely wise and that he had the ability to communicate with wolves. Four wolves were reported to have accompanied him into his battle to regain the throne from Lugaid and that these wolves stayed with him the rest of his life.

## Bleiden

The Celts had wolf warrior bands, known as the "Bleiden" or "wolf." Some sources suggest they engaged in shapeshifting and homosexual initiations. Unlike the Greek and Norse cultures, it was not considered shameful to be the passive or submissive participant in homosexual relations. In fact, accounts of pre-Christian Celtic warriors indicate that many were openly bisexual with both male and female lovers.

## Cu Chulainn

Cu Chulainn was the son of the god Lugh and a hero in Celtic mythology. His name means "Culann's hound" or "the hound of Ulster." He gained his name by killing the blacksmith Culann's dog in self-defense and offering to take its place until a new one was raised. The offer was turned down, but the name stuck. A geasa or taboo was placed on Cu Chulainn that he should not eat dog meat. He is closely associated with dogs rather than wolves. He is said to have been able to go into a warrior frenzy during battle, similar to the frenzy of Norse berserkers. While never actually shapeshifting into a dog or wolf, it is said that in this frenzied state one of his eyes would shrink into his head while the other would grow larger, his jaw would become large enough to fit a man's head, and blood would stream from the top of his head. In one story, the goddess Morrigan confronts him while she is in the shape of wolf. Cu Chulainn is often considered to have been in a homosexual relationship with his friend and companion Ferdiad.

## Celtic Deities Associated with Wolves

**Cerridwen,** was a witch or sorceress in the Celtic tale of Taliesin, she is attributed with owning the Cauldron of Inspiration and with shapeshifting abilities. In modern Paganism, she is considered a Moon goddess associated with inspiration, grain, fertility, pigs, wolves, and cauldrons.

**Crom Cruach,** also known as "Lord of the Mound," may have been a fertility or solar god whose worship was said to have been initiated by a Milesian king named Tigernmas. His name is interpreted variously as bloody, gory, slaughter, corn stack, pile, heap, or mound, and other similar translations. Some (mostly Christian and later) sources suggest that he called for the sacrifice of firstborn babies on Samhain in exchange for milk and grain.[7] St. Patrick is credited with destroying his statue in Ulster. Crom Cruach is often depicted as a gold figure surrounded by twelve figures cast in bronze or stone. It is suggested that he represents the sun and the twelve figures represent the signs of the Zodiac. Crom Cruach may have been worshipped by a wolf warrior band known as the Laignach Faelad.

**Brighid,** is a triple goddess and daughter of the Dagda. She is one of the Tuatha de Danann. Her name means "fiery arrow." She is associated with agriculture,

---

[7] See above.

fire, healing, inspiration, divination, prophecy, knowledge, poetry, and smith craft. Brighid was adopted by Christianity as St. Brigid. Her special holy day is Imbolc on February 1 which marks the beginning of spring and is celebrated with candles. Her sacred animals include cows, ewes, swans, and wolves. Wolves may have been sacred to Brighid because they rule over the dark times of the year. In one story, St. Brigid is said to have tamed a wolf to replace a king's pet wolf that had been killed by an unknowing peasant. She is sometimes depicted with a wolf companion.

**The Morrigan,** is a goddess of battle, war, strife, and sovereignty. Her name means either "Great Queen" or "Phantom Queen." She is one of the Tuatha de Danann. She appears in many forms including as a crow, eel, cow, and wolf. She has a wolf companion. Her connection with wolves is likely due to their associations as a scavenger on the battlefield. The Morrigan took the form of a red-furred wolf when testing and chasing the Celtic hero Cu-Chulainn. She offered her love to him, but he rejected her.

**The Cailleach**, is a crone or hag goddess who personifies winter and the elemental aspects of nature. She is often depicted as an old woman with one eye, bad teeth, and disheveled hair. Her staff is said to freeze the ground and she brings storms. Sometimes she is shown riding on the back of a wolf and waving a magic hammer or wand. She is a protector of wild animals, especially deer and wolves. In some stories, she rewards those who are kind to her when they meet her in their travels.

**Cernunnos,** is a horned god and god of animals, nature, fertility, and eroticism. He is often depicted seated cross-legged, holding and wearing torcs, and surrounded by animals including wolves, stags, and ram-horned serpents. Much of what we know about him is speculative as very little is mentioned about him in early literary sources. Some modern Pagans associate Cernunnos with shamanism and shapeshifting. In one representation of the god found at Val Camonica in northern Italy, Cernunnos stands while a smaller, naked figure with an erection worships the god. Some have taken this to mean that autoeroticism and/or homoeroticism may have been involved in the god's worship.

**Merlin,** is a legendary wizard and Druid who may or may not have been a real historical character. Some historians believe he is an amalgamation of several historical and legendary figures. The legendary Merlin is best known for his associations with King Arthur. The legendary Merlin was a trickster figure, an advisor, and a teacher attributed with magickal powers including knowledge and proficiency in astronomy and astrology; shapeshifting, glamour, and other disguise; prophesy and divination; alchemy; weather magic; and teleportation. In some stories, Merlin took an old grey wolf as a companion during a period in his life where he lived in the woods as a hermit. Some modern Pagans have elevated

Merlin to the status of godhood, while others see him as an ancient god who was diminished with the coming of Christianity. Merlin is especially venerated among Revivalist Druids.

**The Tuatha de Dannan,** "children of the Goddess Danu," are the primary pantheon of deities from pre-Christian Ireland. They are an ancient race of magickal superhumans who invaded Ireland and defeated the native races known as the Fir Bolg and the Fomorians. Eventually the Gaelic Celts arrived and defeated the Tuatha. At that time many of the Tuatha withdrew into the earth, while others went to an island in the West called "Tir Nan Og" or "Land of the Young." The Tuatha de Dannan are often associated with the fey and many had the ability to shape-shift.

# Chapter 6: Norse Varulfur

## Overview of Norse Werewolves

Varulfur is the Norse term for werewolf. The term vargr can refer to either wolves or outlaws. Ulfr is another term for wolves.

Norse mythology is full of tales of wolves and of men changing into wolves, as well as other animals such as bears and boars.

Shape-shifting in Norse mythology and folklore often involves physically taking on the pelt or skin of an animal or taking on the hamr or shape of an animal while in a shamanic state. Taking on a wolf shape is known as vargshamr or ulfhamr. In other cases, spells are cast so that people resemble wolves or other animals.

In cases where humans were transformed into animals as part of a curse, the curse is often ended by removing the animal pelt whereupon the pelt is burned to prevent it from being used again.

The Norse Volsunga Saga includes stories of wolves and werewolves throughout the entire narrative. The Volsungs are also sometimes called Ylfingar, translated as "wolflings."

Other sagas featuring werewolves include the Trojumanna Saga (which includes references to wolf warriors), Gibbons Saga, Ulfhams Saga, Tiodel's Saga, and several others.

Men who practiced a feminine form of Norse magick and shamanism called Seiðr were considered ergi. Practices within Seiðr include soul travel, shapeshifting, and sex magick.

Besides the wolf, Norse shapeshifters also frequently shifted into bears including bear warriors known as berserkers.

Ritual homosexuality may have been involved in initiations into Seiðr, into the cults of certain gods and goddesses, and into wolf and bear warrior bands.

## The Terms "Ergi" and "Argr"

The terms "ergi" and "argr" are terms used in insult to suggest someone is effeminate or unmanly. Ergi is a noun for an effeminate man and argr (sometimes ragr) is an adjective to denote someone who is effeminate or unmanly. These terms also suggested that one was the passive or receptive person in homosexual anal intercourse. Similar to Greek customs it was generally considered taboo to be on the receptive end of homosexual anal intercourse between men of otherwise equal status. It was okay, even worth bragging about, to be the active partner in such cases. It was less of a taboo to be the receptive partner in homosexual relations between men if one was lesser in age, rank, or social status.

One Norse wolf charm (translated by M.R. Gerstein) interchanges the root term for wolf (vargr) and the root term for effeminate men (argr) proclaiming:

> *Call me varg*
> *and I'll be arg*
> *call me golden*
> *and I'll be beholden.*

## Sigmundr and Sinfjotli

The story of Sigmundr and Sinfjotli from the Volsunga saga involves a father and son. In their travels, they find and steal wolf pelts from a hut in the forest. These are magic pelts that transform men into wolves and the pelts can only be removed after wearing them for ten days. Sigmundr and Sinfjotli put on the pelts and live as wolves for the ten day term. The two decide to travel on their own, but agree to howl if either becomes engaged in a battle with more than seven men at one time. Sinfjotli, the son, disregards their agreement and fights eleven men on his own and is injured in the fight. Sigmundr becomes angry at his son's pride and arrogance and bites Sinfjotli in the throat, mortally wounding the youth. A raven, messenger of Odin, brings a leaf that heals and revives Sinfjotli. At the end of ten days they remove the pelts and burn them.

Some have suggested that this episode is related to an adolescent rite of passage where Sinfjotli goes into the forest with his father to learn to the live in the woods and how to endure hardship. In the process, he trains as a warrior, endures a trial, and comes to learn of the animal nature within him. Doing so brings him closer to the wolf totem of his clan and to the god Odin who is a patron god of the clan associated with warriors and with wolves.

## Gudmundr and Sinfjotli

In one of the Norse Eddas, the warrior / sorcerer Sinfjotli accuses his opponent Gudmundr, a Norse King, before battle calling him an "argr" and suggesting that Gudmundr is effeminate and unmanly. Sinfjotli continues suggesting Gudmundr is a whore who offers himself up to other warriors for their pleasure. Sinfjotli goes so far as to insinuate that all of Odin's warriors (the einherjar) in Valhalla fought over the right make love to Gudmundr. Sinfjotli goes even further to boast that Gudmundr is pregnant with nine wolf cubs and that he, Sinfjotli, is the father. Sinfjotli was a sorcerer who is described as being Ylvingar or "wolf's kin" and who sometimes takes the form of a wolf. This story is often used to suggest that only passive anal intercourse was taboo among the Norse. If it was taboo to be the active partner, it is unlikely that Sinfjotli would insult Odin and his warriors by suggesting they would make love to Gudmundr or incriminate himself by claiming to be the father of Gudmundr's wolf cubs.

## Ulfhednar, Vargr, and Berserkers

The Norse wolf warrior bands were called the Ulfhednar and also the Vargr - meaning wolf coated men and wolf warriors respectively. These Norse warriors wore wolf skins when they entered battle.

More well-known than the Ulfhednar and the Vargr, were the Berserkers. These were Norse warrior bands who wore bear skins into battle and took on the bear as their totem. Often these bands consisted of twelve warriors who took on names related to bears, such as Bjorn. They were said to fight with an uncontrollable rage and fury, which may have been trance induced. Their state of mind was said to be frenzied, wild, and deranged and this is where the term "berserk" comes from. They were said to be very strong and highly resistant to pain. Some theories suggest that these berserkers gained their inhuman powers from psychoactive drugs or the ingestion of bog myrtle, which was one of the main spices used in Norse alcoholic beverages.

These warrior bands are closely related to the Norse God Odin. Initiations into these warrior bands may have involved a mock battle where the initiate fights and subdues a wolf or bear and drinks its blood to take on its power, as well as learning to live in the wilderness as their wolf or bear totem (such as in the story of Sigmundr and Sinfjotli). Some have suggested these initiations may have included ritual homosexuality between warriors and initiates. This could have been similar to Greek homosexual military and civic rites or it may have been an initiation into the cult of Odin or into the practice of Seiðr which have both been alleged to include homosexual rites.

A blood brotherhood initiation rite known as the Jardarmen rite may have involved initiatory homosexuality between Norse elders and youths similar to ancient Greek rites. This rite was used to initiate members into Norse warrior bands such as the Vargr. As such it could provide a direct link between the homosexual ergi and wolf / bear warrior clans. In the ceremony, young male initiates passed through raised strips of turf, known as "earth torques". Instead of being a metaphor for the vagina or womb, it has been suggested by at least one scholar[8] that the "earth torques" may have symbolized anal sex and that the initiates might have participated in communal sodomy to ritualize their entry into

---

[8] Margaret C. Ross in Hildr's Ring: A Problem in the Ragnarsdrapa, Medieval Scandinavia 6. 1973.

adulthood and warriorhood. In Norse culture, torques came to be a symbol of ergi behavior[9]. The gesture of forming the hands into the shape of a ring or torque suggested that the person making the symbol had the power to cause an on looking male to submit to anal intercourse. Odin is alleged to have made this gesture toward Thor implying he could have Thor any time he wanted.

## Troll Women and Wolves

In Norse mythology, including the Poetic Edda, troll women are frequently associated with wolves. Troll women living in the "Iron Wood" forest of Járnviðr east of Midgard gave birth to both giantesses and giant wolves. The troll women living there are called "Járnvidur." Troll women are often depicted riding wolves.

## Norse Deities Associated with Wolves

**Fenris,** also known as Fenrir, Fenrisúlfr, Hróðvitnir, and Vánagandr, is a giant wolf in Norse mythology. He was the eldest son of the trickster god Loki and the giantess Angroda. A prophecy claimed that one day the wolf and his kin would aid in the destruction of the world at Ragnarok. As Fenris grew larger and larger the Norse gods decided to do something about him. At first they locked him in a cage where he was fed and cared for by Tyr, the Norse god of war. When Fenris outgrew the cage, the gods decided to chain him. In order to do so they tricked him and challenged him by claiming he wasn't strong enough to break the chains. Once they chained him, he broke through even the strongest chains as if they were cobwebs. After this, the gods decided that only a magic chain could restrain the wolf. The gods had the dwarves make a magic chain called, Gleipnir. It was a thin, soft, ribbon made from the footstep of a cat, the roots of a mountain, a woman's beard, the breath of fishes, the sinews of a bear, and a bird's spittle. The gods again challenged Fenris, but he became suspicious since the new chain looked so feeble. Fenris finally agreed to the test, but only if one of the gods would place their hand between his jaws as a sign of good will. After much deliberation, Tyr volunteered, and the gods chained Fenris with Gleipnir. No matter how hard he tried, Fenris could not break free from the thin cord. The gods would not set Fenris free so he bit off Tyr's hand. As the story goes, Fenris remains chained to a rock within the earth with a sword placed between his jaws to keep him from biting. When Ragnarok comes, Fenris will break his chains and join in the battle against the gods. At that time, he will devour Odin and be killed by Odin's son, Vidar.

Fenris had two children, **Sköll** (meaning treachery) and **Hati** (meaning Hate). They chase Sol (the Sun) and Mani (the Moon) who are riding chariots across the sky. Whenever there is an eclipse it is said that one of these wolves

---

[9] Possibly related to male sacrifices to the goddess Freyja.

has briefly captured Sol or Mani. According to the mythology, these wolves will devour the sun and the moon at Ragnarok.

**Odin,** is the head of the Norse Aesir gods. He is considered the father of both the gods and mankind, and is sometimes known by the title All Father. Odin is a god of magick, knowledge, wisdom, and wit. Odin has two pet wolves named Geri and Freki both names meaning "the ravenous" or "the greedy one." These wolves were considered good omens. Odin was known to cross-dress and practiced a feminine form of magic called Seiðr.

**Freyr,** is a Norse solar and phallic fertility god of the Vanir gods. Although presumably heterosexual himself, Freyr was worshipped in his phallic aspect, by gender variant male priests. These priests wore feminine attire and rang bells. They also assumed the passive role in homosexual fertility rituals – a sacred marriage between themselves and the god Freyr. By surrendering themselves to passive intercourse, they became a channel for the divine. These priests performed a feminine form of magic called, Seiðr – associated with Freyr's sister Freya. They also performed shape shifting rites in boar masks. Some of these men were said to undergo a gender transformation every nine nights. At that time, they would go out hunting men in the same manner as a werewolf might hunt victims. Other such gender variant priests would undergo shamanic or astral journeys in the form of animals, particularly the falcon.

**Loki** is a cunning trickster god in Norse mythology and often plays the role of antagonist to the other gods. He is the father of the great wolf, Fenris. Loki had the ability to change his gender and his shape. He is depicted as sexually progressive compared to the other Aesir gods. In one story, Loki took the form of a mare, became pregnant, and gave birth to Odin's eight-legged horse Sleipnir. In the Norse tales, Loki also shapeshifted into a she-wolf, a salmon, a seal, a fly, and an elderly woman.

**Skadi** is a giantess and goddess of the winter, bow hunting, snow shoes, and skiing. She lives in the highest mountains where the snow never melts and she is seen in a more benevolent role than most giants and giantess. She once married the god Njord, but things didn't work out and they parted ways. She is associated with wolves as animals of the winter and she is sometimes called "Sister of the Wolves."

# Chapter 7: Werewolves in the Middle Ages

## Overview of Werewolves in the Middle Ages

In addition to the well-known witch trials of the Middle Ages, there were also werewolf trials.

Those accused of being werewolves were typically men. Accused witches were both men and women. Ratios varied by region, with Catholic regions more likely to have larger numbers of men accused of witchcraft.

Wolf charming and wolf riding were among the charges laid against accused witches during the European witch and werewolf trials.

Women were sometimes associated with shapeshifting abilities. Usually female witches were believed to shapeshift into cats and hares, though some "manly" women were believed to shapeshift into wolves.

Werewolves usually became werewolves through some combination of a supernatural pact, spell craft, the pelt of a wolf, and a magickal (psychoactive) ointment similar to witches' flying ointments.

Werewolves were often associated with social and sexual deviancy including sodomy.

## Werewolf Trials

In Europe, people believed to be werewolves were persecuted along with those believed to be witches. The European witch trials ran from the 15th through the 18th centuries and peaked in the late 16th and early 17th centuries.

Those accused of being werewolves were typically men. Accused witches were both men and women. Ratios varied by region, with Catholic regions more likely to have larger numbers of men accused of witchcraft. There were differences in the types of magick men and women were accused of. Women's magick was generally conceived of as more mysterious and malevolent than men's magick. Women's magick included spirit contact and working with demons, spell casting, mixing poisons and flying ointments, love magick, harming or helping with dairy and butter yields, and benevolent and malevolent magick related to childbirth. Men's magick was perceived as more practical and protective. Men's magick included acts to protect the family and livestock, as well as to heal disease in both humans and livestock; to promote agricultural yields; to affect the weather; to increase material wealth; to protect from violence and war; and to bring luck in hunting.

Men accused of being witches and werewolves were often, but not always, a part of a marginalized group. They may have been poor beggars or vagrants. They may have been physically or mentally handicapped. They may have been at the margins of youth or old age. They may have been of questionable masculinity. In the Middle Ages this included violations of masculine virtue such as selfishness, greed, drunkenness, adultery, or failure to provide for one's family or to go to church regularly. Many accused male witches were further feminized during prolonged periods of interrogation and torture. Even if they started with a strong constitution, they eventually broke and were viewed as weak-minded and womanish. Herdsmen were especially suspect. They spent their time in constant contact with animals and nature which gave them a seemingly supernatural advantage when it came to healing animals and predicting weather. Blacksmiths were also suspect because they worked with fire which led to the belief that they possessed magickal powers.

Men accused of werewolfery were often accused of some form of social or sexual deviance. This included accounts of rape, incest, sodomy, murder, savagery, and cannibalism.

## Flying Ointments, Lycanthropic Salves, and Magick Spells

Werewolves usually became werewolves through some combination of a supernatural pact, spell craft, the pelt of a wolf, and a magickal (psychoactive) ointment similar to witches' flying ointments.

Supernatural pacts were often made with "the devil" or with a man wearing black. These supernatural agents were often encountered in the woods or at a crossroads.

Spells were used by many to become werewolves. These spells were accompanied by the use of a belt or other device made from the pelt of a wolf, the brewing of foul herbs, and the application to the naked body of a lycanthropic salve or ointment. These brews and ointments contained psychoactive plants and herbs that would be absorbed through smell and through the skin respectively. The brews were not actually consumed but breathed in. Ingredients included such things as bat's blood, the fat of a cat, camphor, aloe, poplar leaves, soot, opium, henbane, hemlock, deadly nightshade, aconite, and aniseed. The modern werewolf should beware as many of these ingredients are poisonous.

The ingredients used in lycanthropic salves are nearly identical to those used in the witches' flying ointments that witches used to "fly" to their sabbats. The major difference was the intent of the person applying the salve or ointment. These ointments had hallucinogenic effects which led those using them to believe they were flying or to believe they were becoming werewolves based on their expectations and the power of suggestion. In some cases, they even acted out their hallucinations in the real world going about and acting as wolves do -- for good or ill.

## Shapeshifting Witches and Familiars

Women were less often accused of being werewolves and more often accused as witches that could shift into the shape of cats or hares. One pamphlet printed in Augsburg in the early 1590s describes those women who were werewolves as "manly women." These women were alleged to attack and devour men, boys, and cattle, as well as to drink their blood and eat their brains.

Familiars are supernatural guides that are supposed to assist witches, especially new witches, in their magick. Most of these guides take on the form of animals, though sometimes they appear human. They are sometimes thought to be shapeshifting demons or fae creatures and they could be malevolent or benevolent depending on whom they served. Familiars are sometimes perceived as an astral double of the witch that can be sent out to gather information or take action in the world while the witch rests in a shamanic trance state.

## Wolf Charming and Wolf Riding

Some alleged witches in the Middle Ages were also accused of wolf-riding or wolf-charming. Wolf charming involved selling charms to either ward off wolves or the contrary to malevolently cause wolf attacks. In German folklore, this charm against wolves is known as Wolfssegen. Charms to cause wolf attacks are known as Wolfbann. Those who offered these charms were known as Wolfssegner and Wolfbanner, respectively. The Wolfsegner, also known simply as Segner, were typically poor, elderly men trying to make a living by selling these charms. During the witch trials, many of these men were tried and executed as witches or werewolves.

While "wolf riding" is mentioned in a few of my sources as something witches were accused of, my research was unable to come up with a definition of the term. Wolf riding may have been literally riding wolves like a horse, it may have meant "riding" and controlling wolves through some form of shamanic soul travel, or it may simply be another term for wolf charming.

## Werewolf Cases Involving Sodomy and other Sexual Deviance

At least a few of the werewolf cases involved allegations of sodomy. Loosely defined, sodomy includes anal and oral sex, bestiality, and even non-procreative heterosexual sex and therefore sodomy isn't necessarily confined to homosexual acts.

The English Buggery Act of 1533 was England's first civil sodomy law. This act defined buggery (later to be defined as sodomy) as any "unnatural sex act against the will of God and man." This definition was later refined to include anal sex and bestiality. 18th Century European sodomy laws at the tail end of the European witch trials focused on the homosexual aspect of sodomy and that may have been how sodomy was perceived before that time. The punishment for sodomy was typically more severe than that for other crimes including rape. Punishment of "sodomites" ranged from public shaming to execution.

A few werewolf cases stand out for including allegations of sodomy and sexual deviance.

## The case of Peter Stumpp

Also known as Peter Stubbe, Peter Stumpf, and the "Werewolf of Bedburg", Peter Stumpp was a German farmer accused of killing, cannibalism, and sexual deviancy in the late 1580s. Stump or stub may have been a nickname referring to his left hand being cut off. It was alleged that his front left paw was cut off while he was in the form of a werewolf and that his missing hand as a human was proof of his transformation. Others have suggested that stump or stub may have referred ironically to his sexual deviance and by inference to a short penis. Some French werewolves were said to have short "tails," which may have been slang or a metaphor for other bodily parts.

Under torture, Stumpp confessed to practicing black magic and that the devil had given him a magic belt that allowed him to transform into a wolf. He further confessed to the murder and cannibalism of fourteen children and two pregnant women and to having intercourse with a succubus sent to him by the devil. Stumpp was also accused of incest with his daughter and with a distant relative. His crimes may have included rape and bestiality.

On October 31, 1589, Stump was tortured and executed for his crimes, beheaded, and then burned on a pyre along with his daughter and mistress. At his execution site, local authorities erected a pole with the figure of a wolf on it where they placed Stumpp's head as a warning to others against such crimes.

## The Case of Hans Poeck

Officially known as Johan Martensen van Steenhuijsen, Hans Poeck confessed voluntarily to his crimes without torture. He even demanded a float test to prove he was a werewolf. Dunk tests and float tests were typically used in witch trials.

Hans claimed that after a leg injury three years before his trial that he had met a man in black while walking and asked a man for food. The man, alleged to be the devil, said he would give Hans plenty if he would renounce God, which he did. The man gave Hans a magic cloth that granted him success in all his endeavors. Poeck bewitched people and animals by striking them with the cloth. During that time, Hans also began "walking as a wolf." He was able to become a wolf by putting the cloth on his head. He also claimed to have a belt that assisted in his shapeshifting. Hans' nickname "Poeck" may have indicated participation in homosexual acts. The Dutch term "poekelen" means to carry something or someone on one's back. This may have been another instance of slang or a metaphor referring to homosexual acts.

Hans was hanged or strangled and then burned at the stake.

## The Case of Peter Kleikamp

Another case featuring a man named Peter Kleikamp actually started out with allegations of sodomy. Unable to prove these allegations, the prosecutor switched to allegations of witchcraft which required less evidence. Under torture, Kleikamp confessed to witchcraft and to denouncing God whereupon the devil appeared to him as a black dog. He further admitted to shapeshifting into a wolf, as well as a raven. Kleikamp confessed that as a wolf, he had "bitten" a calf and "shamed" an ox – again metaphors for sexual deviance, in this case bestiality. He also claimed to have had sex several times with a female demon. Hans confessed to attending the witches' sabbat with others and of using a flying ointment on the midnight hour.

The evidence and testimony used against Kleikamp, including his own confessions under torture, were flimsy and circumstantial. Regardless he was charged with witchcraft, tortured, and burned alive on July 13, 1615.

## Chapter 8: Native American Skinwalkers

### Overview of Native American Werewolves

Among many Native American tribes, homosexuality and gender variation are interrelated with shamanism. Shamanism often involves some form of shape shifting.

Many Native American tribes believed that wolves, bears, and other animals are closely related to humans. These tribes often saw the wolf as a brother, other close relative, or ancestor. The wolf was a totem and a protector for many tribes.

Some tribes revered the wolf for its hunting abilities and loyalty to its family or pack. Other tribes saw the wolf as malevolent and antagonistic toward humans.

Some evil witches had shapeshifting abilities and joined in malevolent witch societies. In order to join, the practitioner often had to break some taboo which may have included sexual taboos.

There were also benevolent societies that took on the wolf as their totem and initiated members as wolves.

### Two-Spirits

Homosexual and gender-variant men and women held a special sacred place in many Native American tribes. The two-spirit men wore women's clothing, did "women's work" (such as basket weaving and pottery), and often had relationships and sex with other men. Sometimes they entered into a polygamous relationship as a secondary "wife" to a man who was already married to one or more women. The two-spirit women dressed as men, cut their hair like men, hunted and fought like men, and even married other women. In both cases, their status as a two-spirit was initially hinted at by their character, behavior, and occupational pursuits, but usually a dream, ritual, or test confirmed their two-spirit nature.

Two-spirits were revered as sacred and mystical. They were believed to bring good luck and good fortune. They performed special roles in many ceremonies and rituals. Because they were believed to possess both male and female energies, they often resolved conflicts between men and women and also served as matchmakers. Two-spirits were believed to have mystical healing powers and frequently served as healers. They sometimes conferred magical or lucky names on people.

## Skinwalkers

"Skinwalker" is a term used among many Native American tribes to describe people who have the ability to transform themselves into animals to do harm. In some cases, similar to the folklore of other cultures, they must wear the pelt of an animal in order to transform. While both men and women can become skinwalkers, the majority are male. Some believe that only childless women can become skinwalkers. Skinwalkers often become skinwalkers by breaking tribal taboos or by singing curses rather than healing songs. They are said to have the ability to shift into any kind of animal they want. They frequently choose the forms of coyotes, wolves, foxes, eagles, and crows. Besides shapeshifting, skinwalkers are believed to be able to mimic the voices of members of their family, as well as make other human and animal sounds. They also have the ability to read one's thoughts. One doesn't want to look into the eyes of a skinwalker because they might be able to gain some power over you or absorb themselves into your body. Like European vampires, skinwalkers cannot enter a home without an invitation. As witches, skinwalkers enact curses and use charms and powders to assist them in their malevolence. Charms might be made with the use of their victim's hair, personal belongings, or other items associated with the victim. Powders are often made from bones and corpses and may be blown onto the face of their victims or into their victims' homes.

## Medicine Men

Medicine men are beneficial healers and shamans in many Native American tribes. They are able to travel to other spiritual realms and to connect with animals including personal and tribal totems. They may even be seen wearing the skin of their totem. Medicine men could grant blessings and remove curses. Two-spirit individuals often served as medicine men and shamans in their tribes.

## Animism and Wolf Brothers

Animism is a spiritual belief that animals, plants, and even natural objects and forces such as rocks, streams, and storms have souls or spirits. Many Native American beliefs are animistic including beliefs that certain animals such as wolves and bears are closely related to humans. They are equal to humans and are given human traits. They might be considered our ancestors, parents or grandparents, or our brothers and sisters. Animals are sometimes seen as humans wearing the coats or shapes of animals. In addition to this, some animals took on the roles of teachers, guides, protectors, and totems. They might be a personal totem or the totem of an entire tribe or clan. These animals might appear in dreams and vision quests or as signs in the natural world.

In many Native American stories, you will hear animals referred to in familial terms. Wolves and bears might be brothers, whereas spider might be a grandmother. The Tanaina tribe in Alaska believed the wolves were once men and treated them as brothers.

## The Wolf Star

Among some Native American tribes, such as the Pawnee, the star Sirius is known as the "wolf star" and the Milky Way is known as the "Wolf Road." In their creation mythology, the wolf was the first creature to experience death. When the Earth was being created, the Wolf Star was not invited to attend the council planning this great event. In anger, the Wolf Star sent a wolf to steal a bag from the West containing the first humans. When the wolf opened the bag, the freed humans killed the wolf bringing death to the world.

After this incident, the people prayed, skinned the wolf, and made a medicine bundle. They breathed life into the bundle and waited. After four days, the wolf returned to life and went home to be with his father. The people became known as the "Skidi Pawnee" or the "Wolf People."

## The Navaho

The Navaho people (also known as the Dineh) respect wolves to this day. In their traditional hunting ways, the Dineh shamans and hunters would pray, fast, and make vigils in sweat lodges before hunting. They would symbolically change from humans into wolves to carry out their hunts. During this time they spoke a sacred hunting language and made sacrifices to the Black God, the god of game animals. After the hunt they would return to the sweat lodge for purification and to resume their lives as humans.

The Dineh also feared some wolves who were believed to be witches in wolves' clothing. Some hatalii, shamans and medicine men, joined in secret societies called the yenotlochi or "four-footed ones." They are believed to change into coyotes, wolves, and dogs at night to do harm to others. They wear wolf and coyote skins and make people sick or blackmail them.

To the Dineh, the arrival of a wolf could be good or bad. The wolf could be a sacred messenger or it could be an evil-doer in disguise.

Before Christianity infringed on their native beliefs in the 1890s, the Navajo recognized five genders including woman, man, and nadleeh who were hermaphroditic either physically or in their gender identities. The other two genders are sub-categories of nadleeh. They are masculine females who took on men's roles and feminine males who took on women's roles. Nadleeh historically had specific ceremonial roles in their tribe and masculine male nadleeh feature in many Navajo creation stories.

Navajo relationships were constructed around gender identity first and sexual parts secondly. A relationship between a man and a feminine nadleeh male would not be considered homosexual, nor would a relationship between a woman and a masculine nadleeh female. A relationship between two men (masculine), two women (feminine), or two nadleeh of the same gender and sex would be considered homosexual and even incestuous.

At least one source[10] suggests that some people became Skinwalkers by breaking cultural taboos such as taboos against homosexuality, which was "frowned upon by Navajo society." It is unclear from the text whether this frowning upon took place before or after the Navajo were Christianized or whether this referred to relationships between same gendered Navajo as mentioned above.

## Makah Wolf Society

Among the Makah tribe, members of the Wolf Society capture new initiates during the winter months. The Wolf Society is a mystical healing fraternity. The members would leave the village for several days. During this time, the initiates would be transformed into wolves through prayers and ritual masks. The chosen initiates were taken to the forests and through magical rituals they were transformed into young wolves. After their initiation and training, the new members of the Wolf Society returned to their tribe with new responsibilities and privileges.

## Naguals

Naguals (also Nahuals) were humans in Mesoamerican folklore who had the ability to change themselves into animals through shamanic practices. This could be an actual physical change or it could be a change in their spirit. Often they changed into donkeys, turkeys, and dogs, but the shapes of more powerful animals such as the jaguar and puma were sometimes used. One's birth date might determine whether one would become a nagual. These people believed that everyone has an animal double. Naguals could be good or evil depending on their personality. Some witches known as Brujo are closely related to Naguals. These witches have the ability to transform themselves into animals at night where they drink blood from humans, cause disease, and cause other mischief. Brujo typically transform into bats, owls, and turkeys.

## Blackfoot

In one Blackfoot legend, wolves save a man from a trap set by the man's two evil wives. The man goes to live with their pack. An elder wolf uses magic

---

[10] **Werewolves: A Field Guide to Shapeshifters, Lycanthropes, and Man-Beasts** by Bob Curran.

to transform the man into a wolf-man. From then on, the man has the body of a man and the hands and feet of a wolf.

## The Quileute

The Quileute tribe from Washington State believe their people descended from wolves. The god Q'waeti' or Q'wati had the ability to transform humans and animals. In the legend, Q'waeti came upon two wolves and turned them into humans. These two humans were the first two members of the Quileute tribe.

## The Inuit

The Inuit believed the wolf to be a benevolent animal that protected humans against evil spirits.

They also tell tales of the Ijiraat, shapeshifters who can transform into various animals including wolves. They do so to deceive and kill lone travelers

## Native American Deities Associated with Wolves

**Coyote** is a trickster god in the Native American folklore of many tribes including the Navajo. Coyote is intelligent but impulsive making him the perfect candidate for a trickster god. As with many trickster gods, Coyote's impulsiveness causes trouble and chaos for both humans and himself, but out of this chaos usually comes some benefit for mankind. Among other things, Coyote is credited with bringing humans fire, daylight, the lunar phases, and the Milky Way. Coyote has shapeshifting abilities and is a coyote in animal form and a man with a mustache while in human form. His magickal abilities include transformation, resurrection, and coyote medicine. Coyote sometimes stands as a hero who helps fight off monsters, such as the Thunderbird. In other stories, his intentions are less than honorable.

The coyote is seen among many Native American tribes as a younger and smaller version of the wolf, or conversely the wolf is seen as a larger, older, and wiser coyote. The Navajo word for wolf is mạ'iitsoh, which translates as "large coyote."

**Chibiabos** is the brother of the cultural hero Manabozho (a Great Hare spirit) in Anishinabe / Algonquin folklore. In some stories he is adopted as a brother by Manabozho rather than being a biological brother[11]. Chibiabos is associated with rabbits and with wolves and is often depicted in a wolf form. He was killed

---

[11] In many ancient cultures homosexual couples referred to their lovers as "brothers" and engaged in "adoption" ceremonies to seal their unions. Rites of blood brotherhood served a similar function. Whether this is the case in this story is unknown.

by water spirits and became a god of the underworld. He is also a god of the sky, wolves, and the spirit realm. He is usually seen as benevolent and kind.

**Malsumis,** sometimes Malsum, is the evil twin brother of Glooscap or Gluskab, a benevolent creator deity. Malsumis might be good or evil depending on the interpretation, though he is generally seen as evil. Some tribe elders suggest Malsumis was corrupted and demonized with the coming of the white man. Malsumis is alleged to be responsible for putting thorns on plants and for giving insects a sting.

**Rhpisunt** is Protector of the Haida Wolf Clan, she was a human woman who married a bear and had human headed bear cubs.

**Wisakachek** is a benevolent shapeshifting deity who gave two brothers from the Fox tribe[12] the ability to change into wolves to hunt. In the story, Wisakachek appeared in human form to the brothers Matchitehew and Kreme while they were hunting. Wisakachek claimed he was hungry and the brothers shared their food with him. Later Wisakachek appeared to the brothers again and asked them how their hunt was going. It wasn't going well and they hadn't caught anything since they'd last seen Wisakachek. Remembering their previous kindness, Wisakachek offered them the ability to shapeshift into wolves. They could use this ability for hunting, but not to hurt humans. As wolves, they were able to capture enough deer to feed the whole tribe. A while later, Matchitehew had a disagreement with another boy and turned into a wolf and killed the boy. As punishment, Wisakachek cast a spell causing Matchitehew to lose his ability to shapeshift at will. Instead he was forced to be a human by day and to transform into a wolf every night. Kreme did no wrong so Wisakachek allowed him to keep his shapeshifting abilities. Matchitehew is considered by many as the "Father of Werewolves" in North America.

---

[12] From the area now known as Wisconsin.

# Chapter 9: Christianity – Wolves in Sheep's Clothing

## Overview of Christian Beliefs about Wolves and Werewolves

Early Christians did not believe a human soul could transmigrate or reincarnate into the body of an animal. Since humans are created in God's likeness, it was sacrilege to believe a human's divine soul could enter something as base as an animal.

In the 12th Century and before, Christian scholars believed that only God could perform the transformation of matter - including the transformation of humans into wolves or other animals. Therefore werewolves could not exist. Anyone who believed they saw or were werewolves were actually seeing an illusion or were otherwise mentally deluded.

In the Middle-Ages it was considered heretical NOT to believe in werewolves. To believe otherwise would invalidate the witch and werewolf trials of the times.

A few saints are associated with wolves.

Some Christian influenced werewolf fiction of the 12th century espouse the idea of the "noble" werewolf who is chivalrous and aspires to Christian ideals.

An act of cannibalism during the First Crusades inspired a renewed interest in werewolves as well as a debate over whether partaking in the Eucharist was actually cannibalism.

## Wolves in Sheep's Clothing

In Christian symbolism, the faithful followers of Christ are considered sheep and Christ is the shepherd. Wolves as predators of sheep are seen as those preying on the faithful. Wolves are considered evil men and devils who are greedy, destructive, and who are out to get innocent believers.

False prophets are also linked to wolves. In the **Dialogue de la Lycanthropi**, written in 1595 by a Franciscan monk named Claude Prieur, one of the book's characters explains "… just as we see wolves at the beginning garbed in a cloak of gentle and tame simplicity; but a little later having discarded this skin of pretense and simulation, it is not possible to recount what damage, what devastation, what cruelty they wreak against the poor sheep. In the same way these false prophets use flattery on simple people, suddenly taking them by the throat in order to prevent them either from praising God, making their confession, or taking their accustomed pasture in the green meadows of the church: because of this our Savior tried particularly to turn us away from them, foreseeing the horrible disaster that they recently carried out against his flock."[13]

The Malleus Maleficarum claims that wolves can either be agents of God sent to punish sinners or agents of Satan sent to test the faith of Christians. Christianity replaced the popular Pagan animal totems of the wolf and the bear with their own animal symbols – the lion and the eagle.

## Nebuchadnezzar

The Bible contains at least one reference regarding the transformation of a human into an animal (not to mention another story about someone's wife being transformed into a pillar of salt). God transformed the Babylonian king Nebuchadnezzar into a wild animal for seven years because of the king's hubris and refusal to acknowledge God's authority. The king was punished to live in the wild driven from men, eating grass, and drenched in dew. His hair grew like "eagles' feathers" and his nails grew like "birds' claws."[14]

## The Augustine Theory of Metamorphosis and the Canon Episcopi

Early Christians believed it heretical to believe in witchcraft or that humans could transform into beasts. They believed that only God could perform miracles or transform matter. Even so, Satan could create the illusion of such things and deceive people into believing they were real. The reincarnation or transmigration of humans into animals was also discounted because Christians believed that humans and human souls were made in the likeness of God. To believe they could be changed into beasts was sacrilege. The two following texts emphasize these beliefs.

**The City of God**, was written by St. Augustine of Hippo in the early fifth century. The book discusses the history of the Catholic Church, the Pagan religions of Rome, and two metaphoric cities – one built on God and love and the other built on greed and selfishness. In the book, Augustine develops a Christian theory on the metamorphosis of men into animals. He proposes that only God can change the true natures of substance, but that demons can change the appearance of things through illusions and trickery. According to Augustine, man's mind and body are not changed in these instances, they only appear to change. Augustine further goes on to promote the idea of what he called a "phantasm." These phantasms were not the souls of humans, but a part of their consciousness that travels in their dreams while their human body remains distinct. These phantasms could take on the forms of animals and appear to others as animals. This theory is similar in many ways to the beliefs of many

---

[13] **Metamorphosis of the Werewolf**, P. 142.
[14] The Christian **Bible**, Daniel, Chapter 4.

cultures where werewolfism was taken on as a form of astral travel, only with Catholic Christian overtones and explanations.

*The Canon Episcopi* is a passage of medieval canon law written around 900 AD that condemned beliefs in witchcraft and werewolfism. This text furthers Augustine's theory. The passage suggests that the alleged night flights of witches[15] and transformations of humans into animals are illusions and visions sent by Satan and not actual material occurrences. Bishops and ministers were given the authority to take every opportunity to eradicate such beliefs from their parishes and to eject anyone practicing these Pagan arts. According to the text, those who believe in the reality of such things have lost their faith and are being deceived by the devil. So not only were these practices condemned, but also the belief that these practices were real.

## The Malleus Maleficarum

**The Malleus Maleficarum**, "The Hammer of Witches", was first published in Germany in 1487. Written by Heinrich Kramer, a German Catholic, the treatise is a handbook on the prosecution of witches during the witch trials in the 16th and 17th centuries. In the discourse, Kramer reverses centuries of Christian belief in witchcraft and human to animal transformation by making it heretical NOT to believe that these things exist. Witchcraft must exist because the devil exists and witches gain their power from a pact with the devil. Witches actively recruit others to become witches. With the devil's help, witches' have the ability to fly and to transform themselves into animals, including wolves. Any change or transformation was still considered an illusion of the devil and was not permanent, and the change could only be made with God's consent. The essay went on to claim that both men and women could become witches, but women were more susceptible. Among the crimes attested to witches were baby killing, cannibalism, casting harmful spells, and having the power to steal a man's penis. The essay concludes by describing how to prosecute alleged witches.

Kramer mainly condemns witches in this work, but in a few sections he talks about metamorphosis of men into beasts and concludes that these are the result of glamour and illusion rather than actual transformations. He continues to hold to earlier Christian beliefs that only God can create or change matter. However, he asserts that demons can acquire the semen of humans and animals to create imperfect vessels to inhabit.

In the book, Kramer also addresses the issue of children snatched by wolves. To Kramer, these are not werewolves nor wolves influenced by witches. They are true wolves possessed by devils and allowed by God to carry out their evil as a punishment for the sin of a community. The devil can only harm or deceive humans with God's consent and permission.

---

[15] Known as the "rides of Diana", referring to the Pagan goddess Diana

## Wolves of Ossory

The wolves of Ossory were touched on in the chapter on Celtic werewolves. In this section, I'll expound on their story in Christian legend. The Christian version of the story is different from the Pagan version in a couple of ways. In the pre-Christian version, male-female pairs were chosen to transform and live as wolves for seven year periods. They served as protectors helping those lost in the woods and helping the wounded. In the Christian version, either St. Natalia or St. Patrick cursed the people of Ossory and their descendants to become werewolves for refusing to give up their Pagan ways and for being antagonistic toward the Christian God and the Christian church. It is said that these people howled like wolves when the Christians preached to them and tried to convert them and that is why they were changed into wolves in seven year cycles.

An additional account of these werewolves is appended to the Christian version of the tale. The story relates the encounter of an unnamed priest with a werewolf on his travels from Ulster to Meath. The wolf speaks to the scared priest and explains that his wife is deathly ill; the wolf implores the priest to perform the last rites for her. The priest is reluctant to perform these rites on the she-wolf fearing that he'd be committing blasphemy. To reassure the priest, the wolf pulls down the wolf skin from his wife exposing an old woman underneath. After this, the priest gave the communion – though more out of fear than out of reason.

## Saint Albeus

Also known as Saint Ailbe and Saint Elvis, Saint Albeus was a 6th century Irish bishop. He is celebrated as one of the four great patrons of Ireland and his feast is celebrated on September 12. Albeus is credited with baptizing another Welsh bishop, Saint David.

Albeus was found abandoned in the forest as an infant. Legend has it that his parents were fleeing King Cronan. The king wanted the baby dead, but instead the baby was placed on a rock where he was found and suckled by a she-wolf. Later in his life a she-wolf was being chased by hunters and it ran to Albeus and he protected her and her cubs. Albeus is said to have had a miraculous death. Before dying he was taken to the faerie world by a supernatural ship. There he learned the secret of his death. Upon returning to the mortal realm, he went back to his diocese in Emly to die and to be buried there.

## Saint Christopher

Saint Christopher was a Christian martyr killed either under the 3rd century Roman Emperor Decius or under the 4th century Roman Emperor Dacian.[16] Christopher's name means "Christ-bearer" and legend has it that his name was derived because he carried an unknown child across a river and the child later revealed himself to be Christ. Christopher is a patron saint of travelers and among other things is also a patron saint of Bachelors.

In Eastern Orthodoxy, Christopher is sometimes depicted as a large cynocephali – a dog headed man. Before his conversion to Christianity, he is associated with a unit of soldiers called the Marmaritae[17] who were reported to be large in stature with the heads of dogs, or the association may have been due to a misinterpretation of the Latin word for Canaanite versus the word for canine. One story promoted by the German bishop Walter of Speyer asserts that Christopher was a cynocephali from the land of the Chananeans. These cynocephali ate human flesh and barked. When he met the Christ child, he repented for his sins, was baptized, and devoted himself to the service of God as a soldier-saint. As a reward, Christopher was given fully human appearance.

Christopher visited the city of Lycia[18] within the Roman Empire and comforted other Christians who were being martyred there. Christopher refused to sacrifice to the local Pagan gods and was brought before the local king. The king tried to tempt Christopher with women and riches, but he refused to compromise his beliefs.[19] Eventually Christopher was beheaded for his beliefs and became a martyr.

## Saint Francis of Assisi

Saint Francis of Assisi had a particular affinity for nature and animals. For a time he lived in the city of Gubbio that was under frequent attacks from a wolf that killed and ate both animals and humans. Francis set out to find the wolf. His companions in the journey abandoned the quest out of fear, but Francis continued on until he found the wolf and brought it back to town. Francis realized that the wolf was only attacking and eating people and animals out of hunger. He made a pact between the wolf and the townspeople. The wolf would cease the attacks if the people would feed it regularly. He also made an

---

[16] There is some confusion due to the similarity of the names.

[17] As noted in other chapters, wolf warrior bands (the Marmaritae seem to fit this description) often employed homosexual initiations and rites of passage as part of their traditions.

[18] Note the similarity to the Greek persons and cities of Lycaon and Lykaia associated with wolves.

[19] The Girl's Guide to Werewolves (P. 20) suggests that Christopher had an aversion to women.

agreement with the town's dogs that they would not attack the wolf. As a final show of faith, Francis blessed the wolf.

## Saint Hubert

St. Hubert was the Bishop of Liege[20] in the early 8th century. He was the patron saint of hunters, archers, dogs, mathematicians, opticians, and metalworkers. Hubert is believed to have originated the idea of ethical hunting practices. He promoted the idea that as God's creatures animals deserve compassion. He suggested that hunters should shoot and kill animals humanely and should shoot older and sick animals first and never female animals with young or males in their prime breeding years.

Devotions to Saint Hubert were made from people seeking to cure werewolfism. An item known as Saint Hubert's Key was used to cure rabies and lycanthropy. The charm, crafted in the shape of a metal nail, cross, or cone was heated and pressed to the area where the victim was bitten. If this action was taken soon enough, the heat from the key might cauterize the wound and kill the rabies virus or protect one from becoming a werewolf. These keys can also be found inside house doors or hung on house walls to protect residents against werewolves. St. Hubert is also called upon to bless weapons used to hunt werewolves, especially items made of silver.

## Guillaume de Palerne

The story of Guillaume de Palerne depicts the 12th century ideal of the noble and chivalrous werewolf with Christian ideals. The story centers on a prince of Sicily named Guillaume, and his werewolf protector, Alphonse. In the story, the king's brother is plotting to kill the four year old prince so that he can inherit the throne. Before this can happen, the young prince is snatched up by a wolf. All those around believe the wolf is going to eat the child. Surprisingly, the wolf takes the child into the forest and takes care of the prince's every need. One day while the wolf is out searching for food for the boy, a cowherd finds Guillaume and takes him home. When the wolf, Alphonse returns, he panics to find the boy missing and begins to search for him. Alphonse tracks the boy down and is relieved to discover he's being cared for by the cowherd and his wife. The wolf is not seen for several years.

In the interim, we learn that Alphonse was also a prince from Spain. His mother died in childbirth and his stepmother is a sorceress who turned him into a wolf so that her own son could inherit the Spanish throne. The stories of the two princes are similar and intertwined. Throughout the story the werewolf Alphonse appears when Guillaume is in need, as if the werewolf were a guardian angel or other agent of the Divine. Alphonse brings Guillaume food and drink

---

[20] A city in Belgium.

and protects him and those he is with from harm. Later in the story, Alphonse is reunited with his father and step-mother. Through his actions they are able to determine that this is indeed the lost Spanish prince. After he attacks her, the step-mother repents, begs his forgiveness and mercy, and transforms him back into a human. After this, he reveals Guillaume's identity and Guillaume regains his kingdom.

## The Eucharist

Since the topic of cannibalism is frequently associated with werewolves, it is interesting to note debates over the Eucharist in the 12th Century. In 1098, an incident of cannibalism took place in the First Crusade. After a siege in northern Syria in December of that year, Christian crusaders ate the flesh of the Saracens who died in the battle. The act of cannibalism was explained as a result of extreme famine in the region. Reports of the incident traumatized many Christians of the day and fueled a renewed interest in werewolves, as well as a debate over the Eucharist. In Catholic teachings on transubstantiation, the bread and wine consumed are literally believed to become the flesh and blood of Christ. Many Christians of the time became concerned that they were committing cannibalism when receiving the Eucharist.

# Chapter 10: Wolf Warrior Bands and Wolf Cults

## Overview of Wolf Warrior Bands and Wolf Cults

Typically these bands consisted of young men who lived in the wilderness "as wolves".

The most commonly affiliated animals in Indo-European cultures were wolves, dogs, and bears. Other animals included boars and horses.

These were not just warriors, but cultic brotherhoods with spiritual and warrior functions who worshipped the "wolf god" or a god associated with the particular animal that was revered by the band. Often there was a "wolf goddess" or a goddess associated with wolves who was also revered.

Initiations often involved homosexuality and dressing as wolves (or other animals); there was frequently a cannibalistic aspect, as well.

Warrior bands are frequently associated with the "Wild Host" or the "Wild hunt." These were processions of the "dead", demons, ghosts, werewolves, and other spirits that took place at particular holidays during the year.

## The story so far

I've already mentioned a number of these warrior bands and myths in previous chapters. Here I'll elaborate more on why these fit into the schema of wolf warrior bands and wolf cults, and I'll introduce a few more of these wolf bands and cults.

## Overview of Wolf Warrior Bands

In many European cultures, young men took part in cultic warrior bands that involved animal reverence, shapeshifting, and homosexual initiations. These warrior bands existed in ancient Greece, Rome, the Celtic and Norse lands, Germania, and even extended into India, Asia, and other places. The most common animals associated with these warrior bands were dogs, wolves, and bears. Horses and boars were also relatively common. These bands were not simply gangs, nor were they strictly military troops. These bands held both military and religious-spiritual significance.

Usually these cultic bands were entered by young men at puberty and they remained until they officially became adults. The young men in these bands were unmarried; had no land, no herds, and no wealth. They had no armor, shields, nor weapons either, and they fought naked except for animal skins and body paint. They lived outside of society in the forest and outside the boundaries of villages, cities, and towns. They also lived outside of societal laws. Learning to live off the land and away from the conveniences of civilization was part of their rite of passage.

Initiations and rites of passage into these bands usually involved the youth ritually transforming into a predatory animal using animal pelts and honoring a wolf-god (and sometimes a wolf-goddess) or a deity associated with wolves. These initiations frequently involved initiatory homosexuality, as well. In many cultures, it was believed that an older, more experienced warrior could pass on his virtue, strength, and virility to a younger male by being the active partner in anal or oral sex. Initiations often involved hunting, killing, or sacrificing their totem animal or some other act of bravery and skill. Members of these warrior bands frequently engaged in rites of blood brotherhood with the other members in their groups.

These animal warrior bands served as guerilla troops in battle and were said to be fearless and immune to pain. They fought in ecstatic states brought on by intoxicants, war dances, and battle songs. These ecstatic states weren't just brought about for battle. These brotherhoods often had leading roles in religious festivals and they may have used their ecstatic techniques privately and in secret rites to effect consciousness raising. Besides battle, these brotherhoods were associated with prophecy and poetry. Among the Celts, there is some suggestion that they may have been taught by Druids during the winter months. [21]

Membership in smaller bands often consisted of multiples of three with 9 and 12 warriors being common. Larger armies came in multiples of 50 with 50 and 150 being common. When they went into battle they may have communicated both nearby and across long distances with wolf howls.

## The Wild Host / The Wild Hunt

In many cultures, these warrior bands were associated with something called the Wild Host or the Wild Hunt. These were cultic processions that usually took place near the winter solstice or the beginning of the winter months.[22] Parades of armed men, men on horseback, dogs, wolves, werewolves, demons, ghosts, fairies, and men wearing black passed through villages and towns. Ordinary folks who were in the path of the convoy might be kidnapped. Frequently, the Host or Hunt was led by a wolf god or goddess, including the god Wodan.

While these Hosts and Hunts were somewhat frightening, they were also anticipated as they were believed to bring prosperity, luck, and good crops and

---

[21] See **The One-eyed God: Odin and the (Indo-)Germanic Mannerbunde** by Kris Kershaw.

[22] The late-Autumn / early-Winter processions later turned into what we now know as Halloween.

herds in the coming spring. Other accounts suggested that they were harbingers of catastrophe such as war, plague, or death.

**Below is an incomplete listing of Wolf (and other animal) Warrior Priesthoods for select European cultures:**

<u>Ancient Greece</u>

**Greeks of Arcadia**

I've already mentioned the Greek initiations and festivals associated with wolves at Mount Lykaion ("Wolf Mountain") in ancient Arcadia. These stories have the hallmarks of this being a wolf warrior priesthood. Young men were initiated in rites of passage where they "became" wolves for a period of time living wild in the wilderness. They worshipped and made sacrifices to the wolf aspect of Zeus known as Zeus Lykaios. Homosexual initiations were implied as part of their rites of passage. For more detail, please refer to Chapter 2: Greek Lycanthropes.

**Apollo Lykeios**

Apollo Lykeios[23] was associated with young initiates living in the woods like wolves. He was the god of honor at an annual initiatory feast that took place in the month of Apellaios. In this role he was seen as the god of the initiation of boys into ephebes[24]. Apollo Lykeios was not the god of youths, but the god of their transition into adulthood. As adolescents, these youth lived in the wilderness and wild untamed places as wolves. Apollo Lykeios' role was to reintegrate these wild youth back into an ordered society through initiation. We see a similar transition in Apollo's own mythos. In earlier times Apollo had been seen as a wilder and darker chthonic god who sometimes brought plagues, pestilence, and war. At some point he transitioned from this young, wild, untamed god into a mature solar god of light, order, healing, prophecy, and artistic expression.

A temple to Apollo Lykeios was founded in Argos. A gymnasium near Athens also bears the name Lyceum in honor of Apollo Lykeios.

---

[23] The term "Lykeios" relates to both wolves and light. Apollo is a god associated with both of these.

[24] Adolescents around the age of 17 or 18 years old.

## Ancient Rome

### Romulus and Remus

The mythical brothers Romulus and Remus may have been associated with a wolf warrior band. Some[25] have suggested that their story may have been related to a homosexual initiation rite into the Cult of Mars. In the story, the twins were abandoned as newborns and were later found and suckled by the she-wolf Lupa. Given that homosexual initiations were common in similar wolf warrior bands and that artifacts have been found depicting Mars surrounded by young male initiates, the story of Romulus and Remus may have been a metaphor for a homosexual initiation rite involving oral sex. Wolves are sacred to Mars, and the initiation into his cult may have involved initiates "suckling" from an older male dressed in wolf skins. "Suckling" would have been a metaphor for oral sex and "milk" would have been a metaphor for semen. It has already been mentioned that in many of these initiations semen was believed to transfer the older warrior's virtue and virility to the young, and that it was common practice in wolf warrior bands and cults for semen to be ritually passed from older to younger warriors through oral or anal sex.

Wolf warrior bands and wolf cults are frequently associated with the founding of cities. The story of Romulus and Remus is the most well-known. Others include the founding of Praeneste by Caeculus who was part of a band wearing wolf-skins; the People of Mount Parnassus[26]; and the Hirpi who will be elaborated in a section below.

### Luperci

The Luperci, "brothers of the wolf", were the priests of the wolf god Faunus. Faunus, also known as Lupercus, is the protector of shepherds and sheep flocks from wolves. The Luperci cult was centered on the supposed cave[27] where the She-wolf Lupa is said to have nurtured Romulus and Remus.

As a priesthood, the Luperci were in charge of the annual festival of Lupercalia celebrated February 13-15. This festival celebrated the founding of their temple on February 15 and also served as a protection, purification, and fertility ritual for the region. Lupercus and Lupa were honored at the festival.

As part of the ritual, salt meal cakes prepared by the Vestal Virgins were burned and the Luperci sacrificed one or two goats and a dog. Then two young Luperci of noble origin were led to the altar and anointed on the foreheads with the sacrificial blood. The ritual knife was then cleansed with wool soaked in milk.

---

[25] The Historian David Greenberg in his book **The Construction of Homosexuality**.
[26] Mentioned in Chapter 2: Greek Lycanthropes.
[27] Known as the Lupercal. A similar term, Lupanar, literally means "she wolves' den" and was an old Roman term for "brothel".

This was followed by a feast and then the Luperci cut thongs from the skins of the animals, dressed in the goatskins (if anything at all), and went around flogging people in the crowds. To be flogged was considered a great honor. The whipping was thought to dispel curses and bad luck and for women it was supposed to ensure fertility and ease the pains of childbirth.

There is an interesting story about why the Luperci run naked. According to a story by Ovid, Pan (the Greek Faunus) came upon Heracles and Queen Omphale sleeping in a tent. Pan desired Omphale, snuck into the tent, and proceeded to have his way with "her." It turned out that Heracles and Omphale had cross-dressed wearing each other's clothes. When Pan reached under "Omphale's" dress, he got a big surprise. After that, Pan insisted that his followers worship in the nude so he wouldn't be surprised this way again. Contrasting this story, Plutarch suggests the Luperci ran oiled up and naked for speed.

## Hirpi

A Roman version of Apollo called Apollo Soranus was worshipped by priests at Mount Soracte. Most likely, this god was the merging of the Greek god Apollo with a local Roman god Soranus. The god had many aspects similar to the Greek Apollo. Apollo Soranus was a chthonic deity associated with wolves, prophecy, purification, and the underworld. The site on Mount Soracte where the ritual[28] was practiced was similar to the Greek Apollo's temple at Delphi in that there were many caves and that intoxicating (even deadly) gases were said to emanate from some of these caves.

The priests of Apollo Soranus were known as the Hirpi[29] and also the "Wolves of Soranus." These priests came from certain families who were exempt from military service due to their religious responsibilities. The cult practiced an annual ritual, though no exact dates for the ritual have been recorded. The ritual involved the priests walking barefoot[30] over hot coals with offerings. The ritual may have taken place in the winter – providing a contrast between the cold weather and the purifying fire. The priests began coming from the mouth of a cave, walked across the embers three times carrying offerings to an altar, and then returned to the cave. The fire and embers represented purification as the priests metaphorically walked between the underworld (represented by the cave) and the world of the living. While the priests performed the ritual, the local community served as an audience. The ritual seemed to be a joyous occasion

---

[28] The ritual and the Hirpi are mentioned by such ancient historians as Virgil, Strabo, Pliny the Elder, and Silius.

[29] Hirpus is the Faliscan term for wolves.

[30] Some applied an ointment to their feet, while others may have relied on a state of ecstasis or their faith in Apollo, to protect them from the burning coals.

despite the underworld associations. The priests represented wolves spiritually and metaphorically, though these priests may not have worn wolf masks or skins.

The origin story for this cult is that priests were making a sacrifice one day and that wolves came and snatched away the sacrificial offerings of meat. Shepherds chased the wolves until they came to the caves of Mount Soracte where gases emanating from the caves killed many shepherds and made others sick with a plague. The people were told the only way to end the plague was for their priests to imitate and live like wolves.

A goddess named Feronia is closely related to the cult. She was worshipped at Mount Soracte in a temple at the foot of the mountain. Her exact associations are uncertain, but she may have been a goddess of liberty and of the Earth and the underworld.

## The Celts

### Faelad

The Faelad were a band of warriors who dressed in wolf skins. They were said to be devoted to the god Crom Cruach.

### Bleiden

The Celts had wolf warrior bands, known as the "Bleiden" or "wolf." Some sources[31] suggest they engaged in shapeshifting and homosexual initiations.

For more information on Celtic shapeshifters and wolf warriors, see Chapter 5: Celtic Shapeshifters.

## The Norse

### Sigmundr and Sinfjotli / Gudmundr and Sinfjotli

Both these Norse myths center around the warrior / sorcerer Sinfjotli who was part of a wolf clan devoted to Odin. These stories might also be metaphors for rites of passage and initiations into this clan. For the full stories, see Chapter 6: Norse Varulfur.

In the first myth, Sinfjotli and his father Sigmundr brave the wilderness and find magic wolf pelts that they put on causing their transformation into wolves. In the story, Sinfjotli is killed, but resurrected[32] with a healing leaf sent by Odin. The story can be seen as an adolescent rite of passage into a wolf warrior clan. We do not know if Sigmundr was the biological father or if he was simply an older father-figure – a mentor. If we assume the latter, we see parallels in Norse and other cultures where an older man mentors a youth. These mentorships

---

[31] Phil Hine.
[32] Resurrection and rebirth are common themes in initiations and rites of passage.

usually involve some form of homosexual relationship and homosexual initiation.

The second myth taken metaphorically, could suggest that Sinfjotli, now grown up, plays the role of mentor and seducer. Sinfjotli accuses his opponent Gudmundr of being "argr" (the passive partner in homosexual intercourse). He suggests that all of Odin's warriors had their way with him and that Gudmundr is pregnant with Sinfjotli's children (nine wolf cubs). As with the myth of Romulus and Remus in Roman culture, the subtext in this myth could imply a homosexual initiation. Perhaps Gudmundr plays the passive role (anal or oral) in homosexual initiation with all the warriors in the clan, and perhaps he must in turn "suckle"[33] the nine wolf cubs who would be younger initiates within the clan.

## Ulfhednar and Vargr

The Ulfhednar and Vargr were "wolf coated" men and wolf warriors among the Norse. These bands were closely related to Odin and may have even been the same band to which Sigmundr, Sinfjotli, and Gudmundr belonged. Their initiations included both shape-shifting and homosexual initiations. They also engaged in blood brotherhood rites[34] which may have included initiatory homosexuality.

## Berserkers

The Berserks were an elite band of warriors in the service of Odin. They would have undergone similar initiation rites to the Ulfhednar and the Vargr. Instead of taking on the wolf as their totem, they took on the bear. Psychoactive drugs or an ecstatic trance may have been the reason for their frenzied state and their immunity to pain.

## Priests of Freyr

The priests of Freyr took on a similar function to the wolf and bear warrior bands, except they adopted the boar as their totem. They served both spiritual and warrior functions. The priests of Freyr are described as feminine men who worshipped Freyr in his phallic aspect and they were said to take the passive role in a homoerotic heiros gamos[35] with the god. These priests performed shapeshifting in boar masks and also were said to undergo gender transformation

---

[33] A metaphor for oral sex.

[34] Including the Jardarmen rite.

[35] A sexual ritual where a priest or priestess symbolically plays out the sacred marriage between a god and goddess.

every nine nights. On those nights they would go out and hunt men the same way a werewolf would hunt its victims.

For more information on Norse wolf warriors, see Chapter 6: Norse Varulfur.

## Unspecified

### Koryos

In ancient Celtic, Germanic, Greek, and other related cultures, young men left their families to form warrior bands. Some of these were the ancient equivalent of street gangs. In order to channel their destructive and mischievous tendencies they were organized into these bands and sent to raid other communities. The youth involved considered themselves part of wolf packs. Many of these included initiation rites where the young men sacrificed a dog or a wolf. These warrior bands likely consisted of eight men and were known as "koryos."

In India, an ancient Sanskrit text called the Rigveda describes a winter rite of passage where young men sacrifice a dog, wear its skin for four years, and after the four years they burn the dog skin and return to society as warriors.

### Heruli

The Heruli, also known as the Heri, Hari, and other variations, were a fierce Germanic tribe of marauders who migrated from Scandinavia to the Black Sea in the 3rd century. In Scandinavia, they were known as härjulvar, translated as "harrying wolves". They joined Gothic groups in raids and invasions of the area during this time. The Heruli took on the wolf as their totem and the wolf god Wodan as their patron. They considered themselves "wolf warriors." The Heruli fought in the nude or with very scant covering. According to the Roman historian Procopius, they were polytheistic and practiced human sacrifice. They were said to practice military, religious, and initiatory homosexuality, and were also accused of practicing bestiality. One of their military tactics was to paint their bodies and shields black and to attack on the darkest nights, such as near the new moon. They would appear to their foes as shadowy, even supernatural, figures in the night. These nighttime raids played on their foes' superstitions and might be the origin for the legend of the Wild Host or the Wild Hunt. Furthering these themes, the Heruli were associated with bogs, marshes, and other liminal spaces.

The Heruli would enter ecstatic states for battle and for composing and reciting poetry, riddles, and genealogies. This state was called "wodnyesse" which meant madness inspired by Odin.

The Heruli wolf packs generally consisted of less than a dozen men, with two older men leading the pack.[36] The average age of these youth was approximately 15 to 20 years of age. They lived in the wild learning survival skills until they reached adulthood.[37] Similar to other Germanic men's societies, the Heruli practiced initiatory homosexuality with older men serving as mentors for younger ones.

[36] As what we would now call the Alpha and Beta.
[37] Often reaching adulthood coincided with the killing of a predatory animal or even another man in battle.

# Chapter 11: She Wolves

## Overview of She-Wolves

When we think of werewolves we typically think of male werewolves. While werewolfism is more of a male thing, there are many stories about female werewolves.

She wolves are often more nurturing than their male counterparts. There are many stories - both mythological and in real life - about female wolves that nurture and suckle lost or abandoned infants in the wild.

Not all female werewolves are nurturing, some are quite predatory and use their dual nature as both woman and beast to prey upon others – particularly men. These female werewolves can be quite sexual.

Female werewolves were popular in Victorian literature and provided an outlet for exploring women's rights and women's sexuality.

The term "werewoman" is somewhat of a misnomer. The term "werewolf" literally means "man wolf", so taken literally "were-woman" means "man-woman." The term were-woman has also taken hold in transgender slang to refer to a man who transforms into a woman at night or possibly once a month on the full moon. This topic is furthered in transgender fantasy fiction and gender transformation erotica that frequently involves a temporary forced transformation of a man into a woman.

## The story so far

In previous chapters I've mentioned Lupa - the she wolf that suckled Romulus and Remus, the legendary founders of Rome. I've talked about the "manly" female werewolves of the Middle Ages and about how only childless women could become Native American skinwalkers. I've talked about Norse troll women and various goddesses associated with wolves. I'll leave these stories in their respective chapters where you can read them again if you like so I can move forward with other tales of female wolves and werewolves.

## Adoptive Mother Wolves and Wolf Children

The story of Romulus and Remus being adopted and suckled by a she-wolf is one of many mythological, historical, and fictional accounts of mother wolves caring for lost or abandoned children. In Greek mythology, there is a story about Miletus who was the son of Apollo and a woman named Akakallis. Akakallis was the daughter of King Minos from the Minotaur story. Afraid of her father and his reaction to the child, Akakallis left Miletus in the wild. Apollo sent she-wolves to nurse Miletus until he was found and raised by shepherds. Miletus grew up to be a handsome young man and Minos, not knowing the boy was his grandson, became enamored with him and wanted Miletus to become his eromenos.[38] Miletus left Crete to avoid this fate and founded the city of Miletus in his own name.

Other myths and legends of heroes being raised by wolves include the Roman myth of Romulus and Remus, the Celtic story of Cormac mac Airt, and Christian folklore related to Saint Albeus.

Wolves aren't the only animals in mythology and folklore who are said to raise human children. Bears, tigers, birds, apes, coyotes, and other animals are said to have maternal instincts toward human children. In the Epic of Gilgamesh, Gilgamesh's companion Enkidu[39] was raised by unspecified beasts. In another story, the Greek huntress Atalanta was said to have been raised by a she-bear.

## The Maras

Scandinavian folklore tells of a race of female werewolves known as the Maras. These women were usually from the peasant and plebeian classes. The mothers of the Maras undertook a ritual to bear children without pain. This ritual involved stretching the membrane of a newly birthed foal between four sticks and passing through it naked. Boys born to these women became shamans and the girls became Maras. Maras were half human and half wolf and their transformations were slow and painful.

## Russian and Slavic Shamanesses

Some Russian and Slavic Shamanesses are reputed to shapeshift while in an astral form. In this form, they are said to fight false sorcerers and dark magicians.

## A Croatian She-Wolf Tale

In one short Croatian tale about a she-wolf, a soldier went into an enchanted mill to sleep. He'd heard tales of a she-wolf who haunted the place. He made a fire in the parlor and then went upstairs. There he bored a hole in the floor so he could watch. A she-wolf came in looking for food and took off her wolf-skin revealing a beautiful woman underneath. She fell asleep beside the

---

[38] In ancient Greece, the eromenos is the younger in a pederastic sexual and apprenticeship type relationship.

[39] Some historians have suggested a homosexual relationship between Gilgamesh and Enkidu.

fire. The soldier came downstairs, nailed her wolf-skin to the mill wheel, and then woke up the woman. She called for her wolf-skin, but it didn't come because it was nailed to the mill wheel. The two married and had children. As the children grew older they inquired about whether their mother was really a wolf. The mother denied it and later they approached their father. He confirmed that she was a wolf and showed them the wolf-skin still nailed to the mill wheel. The mother asked the children where her wolf skin was and they told her. She thanked them for rescuing her and she was never seen nor heard from again.

## Victorian Were-Women Fiction

### The Were-Wolf by Clemence Houseman

Clemence Annie Houseman was an activist in the women's suffrage movement of England in the late 1800s and early 1900s. She was also a writer and illustrator. She wrote "The Were-Wolf" which features a strong she-wolf. The story revolves around twin brothers, Sven and Christian, and the she-wolf, "White Fell" who got between them.

The two brothers were very close and looked very much alike. Swen was the better looking of the two and his "features were perfect as a young god's." Christian was the better hunter and generally the more athletic of the two, though Swen was a faster runner.

On a cold winter night in an isolated community a mysterious woman appears at the house of the twin brothers and their family. The family welcomes the beautiful woman[40] who is dressed in strange clothing. Her clothing is described as "strange, half masculine, but not unwomanly." She wears hunting shoes and leggings, a fur tunic, a white fur cap, and carries a hunting axe. She goes by the name White Fell, because her real name is "uncouth." Swen takes a liking to her. Christian is out hunting and arrives later. On his way home, Christian follows large wolf prints which lead to the door of the house, but no wolf tracks head away from the house. As a skilled hunter, Christian quickly surmises upon entering the house that White Fell is a werewolf. His suspicions are confirmed when their dog acts strangely toward her. The family provides her a room for the night. Christian plans to catch her out and prove that she's a werewolf at midnight. Legend has it that werewolves must take their form as a wolf at that late hour. At midnight, when Christian goes to find her, White Fell has already left as mysteriously as she arrived. Sometime later one of the children, Roll, with whom White Fell had played with and kissed, disappears mysteriously.

Months later White Fell returns. Except for Christian, the family is oblivious of her true nature. Christian confides in Swen about his suspicions, but Swen will hear none of it and warns Christian not to pursue his fantasies. White Fell takes a liking to an elderly woman in the family named Trella and she

---

[40] Hospitality to travelers is an expected custom in many ancient cultures.

kisses her. Later after White Fell leaves, Trella too disappears mysteriously. Christian notes that both family members who disappeared were kissed by White Fell.

Sometime later, Christian is summoned back to the house only to discover Swen and White Fell are a couple. White Fell kisses Swen in front of Christian. Aware of the previous pattern, Christian worries that his brother, Swen, will be the next to disappear.

In the middle of the night, Christian attacks White Fell and chases her through the forest on the cold winter night. The chase ensues through the whole night with both Christian and White Fell taking hits and wounds. Then a final battle takes place between the two.

The next morning, Swen notices that Christian and White Fell are missing and he stumbles upon his brother's footprints. Knowing his brother's obsession with believing White Fell to be a werewolf, Christian fears the worst and follows the trail. All the while, Swen is furious at what his brother might have done to White Fell and his anger continues to grow as he follows the trail and as he finds evidence of the fighting that ensued the previous night.

Finally Swen comes across the body of his brother in the snow and where White Fell should have been was the body of a white wolf. In Christian's death, Swen is filled with regret and realizes that his brother was right and that his brother saved his life. The story ends with Swen carrying Christian's body homeward.

## The White Wolf of Hartz Mountain by Frederick Marryat

"The White Wolf of Hartz Mountain" by Frederick Marryat begins with two sailors Phillip and Krantz who are trying to make their way to the city of Boa. They are on a small sailing vessel that has lost most of its crew. Krantz and Philip are best friends and Philip is going to Boa to meet Amine, presumably a female love interest. To pass the time Krantz tells the story of his family. His story features a she-wolf.

When Krantz was an infant, his father caught his mother cheating on him. In an act of jealousy and fury, his father killed his mother and her lover. Krantz's father then fled their homeland with the three children, Krantz and his brother and sister. They fled from Transylvania to the Hartz Mountains in Germany, a place known for strange and unusual occurrences. There Krantz's father took on the occupation of hunting.

The children led a sheltered life often locked indoors because of their father's fear of being caught. Because of his wife's betrayal, he also distrusted women and would not hire a caretaker for the children. One evening when his father returned home from hunting, a wolf appeared outside their cabin and the father rushed out in pursuit of the wolf. The wolf turned out to be a rare white wolf. Just as the father was about to shoot the wolf, he was distracted by the sound of horns blowing nearby. Searching for the source of the sound, he discovered a man and his daughter who were being chased by pursuers from their homeland in Transylvania. Krantz's father offered the man and daughter shelter for the night in his home. The daughter, Christina, was young, beautiful, and about 20 years old. She wore a white fur coat and white fur hat. After talking, the two fathers discovered that they were second cousins, and the two newcomers decided to stick around for a while. During the stay, Krantz's father asked for Christina's hand in marriage and her father, Wilfred, gave his blessing. Since there were no priests around to officiate the ceremony, Wilfred officiated a simple ceremony between the two, but he insisted that the oath be given to the "spirits of the Hartz Mountains" and not to the spirits of heaven.

After the marriage, Wilfred moved on, but left his daughter wedded to Krantz's father. After the marriage, the children began to notice changes in the woman and strange behaviors. When their father was gone, she beat them and at night they saw her frequently slipping outdoors in her nightgown. They would then they hear the growl of a wolf at their window. Later she would slip back in and wash her face. Sometimes they noticed her stealthily eating raw meat while preparing dinner.

The oldest brother, Caesar, took his father's gun and followed her out one night. A shot was heard and Christina returned bloody and she cleaned herself up while the father slept. The next morning Caesar's body was found mangled as if attacked by an animal. The father buried him, but Caesar's body was dug up again and eaten by wolves in the night.

Later in the spring, the family was outdoors, and the sister, Marcella, returned to the house to cook dinner. Christina went off in the other direction in search of herbs. A scream was heard from the cottage and the family discovered Marcella killed by a large white wolf that fled as they arrived. The father buried her beside what little remained of her brother. That evening Krantz saw his stepmother, Christina, leave the house again in her night clothes. He watched from the window as she dug up Marcella's body. Krantz awakened his father who, expecting wolves, discovered his wife devouring the child's body. He shot her. When he went over to look at the body, he found the body of a large white wolf in her place. The next day, Christina's father, Winfred, returned as a spirit of the Hartz Mountains. He reminded Krantz's father of his oath never to harm Christina and that his children would someday pay the price. Krantz and his father fled to Holland, and shortly thereafter the father died of a brain fever. Krantz believes he is still to perish as a penalty for his father's oath.

At this point, the story returns to Philip and Krantz who are still sailing along a strait in their small ship on their way to Boa. Krantz has a foreboding that he will not live long enough to arrive at their destination. Philip thinks Krantz is delusional from over-exertion and fatigue. Their fresh water supply is dwindling. They sail close to the shore in search of a freshwater spring to replenish their supplies. They find one and they not only refill their water jars, but they take time out to bathe together in the stream before returning to the ship. After bathing, a tiger comes along and snatches up the naked Krantz. It carries him off into the jungle. Philip sits for a long time mourning his close friend who he considers like a brother, and then Philip carries on his journey. Krantz had given Philip his gold just before his death. Philip uses the money and arrives safely at Boa. When he gets there he is not able to find anyone named Amine.

## More Were-Women in Pre-modern Fiction Literature

### The She-Wolf by Saki

"The She-Wolf" by Saki is a humorous short story about a she-wolf - though the story itself doesn't involve an actual transformation. The story involves a man named Leonard Bilister who is more than a little fascinated by magic and the supernatural and who later begins to boast his own powers in "Siberian Magic." Mary Hampton challenges Bilister to change her into a wolf at a bridge party and he replies that "I never knew you had a craving in that direction." The unspoken implication is that she wanted to be changed into a male wolf. She replied "A she-wolf, of course, it would be too confusing to change one's sex as well as one's species at a moment's notice." Bilister warns her not to joke about or mock the "hidden forces." She says not to do it then because it would break up their bridge game, but she challenges him to come to her house the following night to show off his powers.

Mary and another co-conspirator named Clovis, actually have their own bit of "Siberian Magic" in mind to teach Bilister a lesson. They acquire a she-wolf from another colleague who collects wild animals and they set the stage for a fun evening. At the dinner party, Bilister sits around doing parlor tricks with coins and Mary challenges him again to turn her into a wolf. Then she ducks behind some houseplants and out jumps the she wolf. Bilister is befuddled and Mary's husband accuses him, but he denies he changed her. They use sugar cubes to lure the wolf out of the room, but there is still no sign of Mary. All of a sudden she stumbles back into the room and recounts the events that took place in the room from the wolf's perspective including having been given the sugar cubes, which by the way was against her doctor's orders.

Mary congratulates Bilister for turning her into a wolf, but by then it is obvious to everyone in the room that he hadn't performed this feat. Clovis steps up taking the credit for the transformation and says that he has more than a passing knowledge of Siberian Magic. He embarrasses and shows up Bilitis by implying that Bilitis was talking nonsense and only had a "tourist's acquaintance with the magic craft of that region."

# Chapter 12: Gender Shifting in Mythology

## Overview of Gender Shifting

Gender shifting gives one a better understanding of the plight of both men and women and gives one special knowledge and powers as matchmakers and mediators between men and women.

Gender shifting helps male shamans and priests to connect with the divine feminine and can likewise help women to connect with the divine masculine.

Some instances of gender shifting involve males who shift into females in order to "hunt" or seduce other men sexually.

## The story so far

In previous chapters I've mentioned a few stories of gender transformation. I've touched on a handful of gender transformations mentioned in Ovid's Metamorphoses. I've told the Celtic story of Gwydyon and Gilvaethwy who alternated genders when turned into deer, pigs, and wolves as punishment. I've talked about the Norse priests of Freyr and the Norse god Loki who were said to change gender as well as shape. Besides stories of actual gender shifting, I've also shared stories of cross-dressing including the Norse god Odin and Native American two-spirits. I'll leave these stories in their respective chapters where you can read them again if you like so I can move forward with other tales of gender shifting.

## Tiresias

In Greek Mythology, Tiresias was a blind prophet of Apollo who lived in Thebes. He had an extraordinary ability to see and divine the future. His father was a shepherd and his mother was a nymph. Among Tiresias' claimed talents were abilities to understand the language of birds, to divine the future from fire and smoke, and to communicate with the dead.

There are a couple of different stories about the cause of his blindness. Some stories say that he revealed the secrets of the gods and others say that he was blinded for seeing the goddess Athena naked while bathing. In another story, Tiresias mediates an argument between Zeus and Hera about who gains more pleasure from sex since Tiresias has experienced sex as both male and female. Hera claims the man enjoys sex more and Zeus claims the woman does. Tiresias implies that the woman does by saying "Of ten parts a man enjoys one only." Losing the argument, Hera is said to have struck Tiresias blind for his irreverence.

The story of his sex transformation is more straightforward. According to the story, he came across a pair of copulating snakes in his path and he hit them with a stick.[41] The goddess Hera was not pleased with this action and then punished him by turning him into a woman. He is said to have lived as a woman for seven years during which time he became a priestess of Hera, married a man, and had children. Some stories claim that she became a renowned prostitute, as well. At the end of the seven years, she came upon two copulating snakes again and this time left them alone. As a reward, she was released from the curse and transformed back into a man. Because of this story, Tiresias is sometimes associated with the caduceus – Hermes staff featuring two snakes entwined about the staff.

Tiresias appears in a number of Greek stories including the Odyssey and the story of Oedipus.

## The Kitsune

In Japanese folklore, intelligent, supernatural fox spirits known as kitsune are believed to have the ability to shapeshift into humans, as well as to change genders. Kitsune can serve as loyal guardian spirits or they might act as tricksters. Good kitsune are known as the zenko. They are benevolent and are associated with the Japanese god Inari. Inari is an androgynous god of foxes, fertility, rice, tea, Sake, agriculture, prosperity, and success. Malicious, malevolent, and mischievous kitsune are known as the yako. Kitsune are depicted as having up to nine tails. The older and wiser a kitsune becomes, the more tails s/he grows. They are also usually represented with magical jewels or pearls that they carry in their mouths or on their tails. These pearls hold their magical powers and possibly even their souls.

Kitsune are credited with many supernatural traits including the ability to possess humans, generate fire and lightning from their mouth and tails, become invisible, fly, visit people's dreams, and create powerful illusions. Some tales even credit kitsune with abilities to bend space and time, to inspire madness, and to take on fantastic shapes. Some kitsune are said to feed on the life force of humans, usually through sexual contact.

Kitsune have the ability to shapeshift and to gender-shift and can even impersonate the appearance of a specific person. They often take on the forms of young women and elderly men. Regardless of their true gender, kitsune are frequently said to transform into beautiful young women in order to trick men into having sex with them and sometimes even into marrying them. Kitsune wives are often loyal and devoted, but disappear suddenly if their true nature is discovered. Sometimes children are born of these unions and the children frequently inherit extraordinary powers and supernatural abilities. It is common

---

[41] In some versions of the story, Tiresias' indiscretion was not for striking both snakes, but because he struck the female snake.

in Japanese folklore to suspect any woman met alone, especially at dusk or in the night, because she just might be a fox in disguise.

Offerings to kitsune include tofu and sushi.

## Hu Hsien

Almost identical to the Japanese Kitsune is a supernatural creature in Chinese folklore called Hu Hsien. This shapeshifting fox also has the ability to gender shift. Sometimes Hu Hsien falls in love with a human male and he might change into a woman or keep his male form depending on the human's proclivities. Sexual relations with Hu Hsien are a mixed bag. For one thing, he is linked with venereal diseases and for another he drains the chi or life force from his human lover as the relationship grows stronger. On the other hand, men rarely refuse a relationship with Hu Hsien because he brings wisdom and good fortune. He is also extremely sensual. Eventually Hu Hsien must leave his lovers or their life force will be drained completely and they will die.

## Jinn

Jinn are serpentine shapeshifting spirits in pre-Islamic Arabian mythology. They possess the ability to change both shape and gender. Jinn are not immortal, but they are very long-lived and can understand and speak all languages. They were once associated with the cult of the goddess Al-Lat. Jinn are said to be bringers of wealth. Devotees of the Jinn included transgender and homoerotically oriented males known as the Al-Jink and the Mukhannathun. The Jinn are linked to a concept known as Mujun which embraces homosexual desire, transgenderism, and mysticism.

## Cross-dressing Priests and Shamans

The shamans and priests in many pre-Christian spiritual traditions were often transgender, gender variant, or homosexually inclined. In many cultures these individuals were revered for their difference. As liminal beings in-between male and female they were believed to bridge the gap between men and women. Because of their liminality, they were assumed to have the ability to travel between the various realms of existence where they could also bridge the gap between deities, supernatural spirits, and humankind.

As a practical exercise, many shamans and other mystics engage in both shapeshifting and gender shifting. By taking on the form, characteristics, and personalities of animals, plants, and objects, shamans are better able to understand them, to understand their motivations, to predict their actions, and to unlock their secrets. Early and even later shamans took on the pelts of animals and danced in rituals to help ensure a good hunt of the animal in question.

Warriors often took on the pelts of animals to get in touch with the instincts, cunning, and fighting skills of the animals.

Cross-dressing as a form of gender-shifting was (and still is) utilized by shamans and priests for a number of purposes, regardless of their sexual orientations or gender identities. For one thing, cross-dressing allows one to cross mundane boundaries of male and female and to deconstruct one's sexual and gender identity. Deconstruction of identity is a big part of many shamanic traditions. Doing so allows one to get past one's own mental blocks, biases, and assumptions. It allows one to create and act out other identities in the quest for knowledge and magickal power. Cross-dressing priests were sometimes associated with goddess worship. Male priests would take on the dress of women as a way to better connect to a goddess and sometimes to invoke a goddess into possessing their bodies. In some cases, castration was even required of the male priests of certain goddesses. Cross-dressing was also associated with the priests of certain male gods. In some cultures homoerotically inclined priests cross-dressed and engaged in homosexual rituals as a way to connect to a god. Sometimes the priests became consorts to a god through a type of wedding ritual. Other times, they acted as the passive partner in homosexual anal or oral sex and served as a vessel for receiving the "inspiration" and blessing of the god by accepting the semen of another man representing the god.[42]

## Transgender, Cross-dressing, and Androgynous Deities

**Aphroditus** was a male or androgynous Aphrodite in Greek myth associated with the moon. He was depicted with a female shape and wearing feminine clothing, but he also had a phallus. In festivals and fertility rituals honoring Aphroditus, men and women would exchange clothing and act as if they were the other gender.

**Dionysus**, the Greek god of wine, pleasure, and ecstasy is also a patron god of intersex and transgender people. His attributes include the thrysos[43], the drinking cup, and the vine. Dionysus is known as "twice born" because his mother, a human woman named Semele, died during her pregnancy with him.[44] As a result, Dionysus's father Zeus "stitched" the unborn boy into his thigh and fathered

---

[42] Such sacred marriages and the enactment of sacred sexual rites is known as the Hieros gamos. Participants usually act out the union between a male god and a female goddess. Cross-dressing male priests sometimes substituted for a female in the place of a goddess, especially in all male priesthoods. The hieros gamos is often a part of fertility ceremonies and rituals aimed at increasing the fertility of crops, animals, and even humans. Modern LGBT pagans sometimes enact the hieros gamos featuring homosexual and bisexual deities and their same-sex lovers as depicted in their mythologies.

[43] A pine-cone tipped staff.

[44] Hera in her jealousy over Zeus's escapades tricked Semele causing her death.

him to term. Dionysus is credited with the ability to shapeshift and with cross-dressing, a skill he learned so he could avoid the wrath of the goddess Hera. Dionysus is portrayed as strong and virile, but also soft and feminine. His dual nature extends to paralleling the dual nature of wine. He could bring joy and ecstasy or he could bring blinding rage. As a vegetation deity, Dionysus is associated with death and rebirth. In one story, he was ripped apart by the Titans only to be brought back to life by the goddess Rhea. Dionysus's festival was held in the spring when the vines would return to life after their dormancy in the winter months. Dionysus was attended by troops of Mainades[45] and Satyrs[46] sporting erect penises. Dionysus was known to have both heterosexual and homosexual relationships.

**Ganesha** is a popular Hindu god most widely venerated as a remover of obstacles and a god of beginnings. He is often acknowledged at the beginning of rituals and ceremonies. Additionally, Ganesha presides over arts, sciences, intelligence, and wisdom. He is said to protect the powers of the root chakra and kundalini energy which are entered through the vagina and anus. Some have linked Ganesha to homosexual worship involving anal sex. Ganesha is depicted with a human body, four arms, and the head of an elephant. Although he is male in gender, he is portrayed with woman's breasts. He is frequently portrayed sitting in a meditative state holding flowers and riches.

**Hermaphroditus** is an androgynous god in Greek mythology, though he was not always so. Originally, he was born as an incredibly handsome boy to the goddess Aphrodite and the god Hermes. One day he met the nymph, Salmacis, in her pool in the woods of Caria. At this time, he was probably still in his early adolescence. Salmacis lusted after the boy, but he rejected her. Later he thought she had gone and he undressed and went to bathe in her pool. At that point, Salmacis jumped from behind a tree and accosted the boy. While she held him tight, Salmacis prayed to the gods that she and Hermaphroditus would never part. The gods granted her wish by fusing her body with his thus creating a being that was neither fully male nor fully female. This is where the term "hermaphrodite" comes from. Hermaphroditus is depicted with both breasts and a phallus.

The Norse Gods **Odin** and **Loki** have already been mentioned in the chapter on Norse Wolves. Both have been linked to cross-dressing and gender-shifting. Loki was even said to have become pregnant while in the form of a mare and gave birth to Odin's eight-legged horse Sleipnir. Odin practiced a feminine form

---

[45] Wild, ecstatic female worshippers.
[46] Lustful hybrid creatures that had the upper body of a man and the lower body of a horse or goat.

of magic known as Seiðr. Odin and Loki are blood brothers and their relationship has homoerotic connotations.

# Chapter 13: Werebears and Bear Worship

## Overview of Werebears and Bear Worship

A whole segment of modern gay culture takes on the bear as a totem for large, hairy, masculine men.

The bear as a totem is associated with strength, introspection, personal power, and healing, among other things.

Bears are worshipped and treated as deities or ancestors in a number of cultures. In some cultures, bear worship is associated with homosexual rites and semen conservation.

Werebears are usually seen in a more positive way than their werewolf counterparts. They are seen as more nurturing and often as guardians and protectors.

## The story so far

I already mentioned the Berserkers, in the chapter on Norse shapeshifting. I've also revealed how Native American tribes felt a kinship to certain animals including wolves and bears. I'll leave these stories in their respective chapters where you can read them again if you like so I can move forward with other stories related to bears and werebears.

## Gay Bear Culture

A whole segment of modern homosexual men has taken on the bear as their cultural totem so it's only fitting that I devote a section to them. These are not men who wear bear skins to get in touch with the spirit of the bear or try to shapeshift into animals. These aren't men who necessarily or actively take on the bear as a totem animal. Modern gay bear culture celebrates large, hairy, masculine men. Bears might be overweight or muscular, but either way they are large. There's also an overlap between bear culture and the leather community.

Bears are further broken down into sub-categories, many that reference types of bears and other animals. Grizzly bears are extra-large or extra hairy. Polar bears are older bears with white body and facial hair. Black bears, Panda bears, and Koala bears are bears of African, Asian, and Australian descent respectively. Otters are slimmer or less hairy bear types of all ages and wolves are slimmer bears that are sexually assertive, sometimes even aggressive. Cubs are younger or smaller bear types.

The term "bear" was coined as a type for gay and bisexual men in the July 26, 1979 issue of **The Advocate** magazine in an article titled "Who's Who at the Zoo?" The term was later popularized by Richard Bulgar and Chris Nelson in their founding of **Bear Magazine** in 1987.

While gay bears aren't trying to shapeshift into animals, there is a shapeshifting aspect to bear culture in that gay bears are trying to project a certain image of themselves which may or may not fit with reality (the same can be said of drag queens). Some have argued that not all gay bears are as masculine as they appear to be - citing examples of hyper masculine looking bear men who are great at projecting this image until they open their mouth only to reveal a really feminine guy beneath the façade. That isn't the case for all bears, but it is the case for some.

## The Bear as a Totem

Many within the Pagan community and in various native and shamanic traditions take the bear as a totem. The bear is a symbol of strength and introspection. The bear is at the top of the food chain and it's only major predator is mankind. Bears are omnivores. They eat berries, fish, plants, insects, and other animals. Some bears even eat large animals such as elk, moose, deer, and caribou. Because they eat many types of berries, plants, and herbs, bears are associated with healing and medicine. In the winter, bears in cooler climates hibernate – often in caves, logs, or other hidden earthy places. This is what gives them their association with introspection, intuition, the subconscious, and the element of earth. Bears are protective of their territories and of their cubs, and the bear totem is often seen as a strong and powerful guardian. Bears are often loners balancing their time with others and their time alone.

## Bear Worship

The worship of bears is found in many Northern Eurasian and North American native cultures. Some even believe that bear worship goes back to Paleolithic times.

Paleolithic bear worship may have involved the consumption of semen. While women's supply of blood was considered endless due to their ability to menstruate, men's supply of semen was considered limited. Therefore men needed to conserve and replenish their supply. This is similar to Melanesian beliefs[47], and may also be why many traditions surrounding sacred sexuality call

---

[47] Traditional Melanesian rites of passage involve the infusion of adolescent males with semen through both oral and anal sex. This is believed to introduce masculine virility to the youth which allows them to grow body and facial hair, create their own semen, and otherwise become men. Other cultures such as the ancient Greeks held similar rites of passage. The Melanesians were also concerned with the conservation of semen and homosexual sex was

for the conservation of semen. Blood and semen are considered vital life fluids related to one's energy and vitality. Early peoples considered semen and cerebrospinal fluid to be the same thing because they were both white liquids and therefore semen was believed to originate in the brain. Because bears were considered related to humans, the semen and cerebrospinal fluid of bears was considered comparable to that of human males. Efforts to increase or conserve semen among Paleolithic men may have included participation in bear cults, bear hunting, head hunting, cannibalism, and the use of human skulls. One bone carving from this period found at La Madeleine in France seems to confirm this theory. The carving depicts semen gushing from a human phallus and entering the head of a bear.

Among the Nivkh of Russia an annual bear festival was celebrated in the middle of the winter. Bears were believed to be the ancestors of the tribe manifesting in bear form. Bears were captured, raised, and treated quite nicely for several years by local women. The bears were offered a luxurious banquet and a shaman would preside over the festival. At the end of the festival, the bears were killed and eaten. It was believed that the bear would return to the gods of the mountain and that they were happy with being honored in this way. As a result, they would reward the Nivkh with bountiful forests.

Pre-Christian Pagan Finns believed that bears came from the stars and that they could reincarnate. In other words, there was no harm done by killing and eating them[48]. After a successful bear hunt, the bear would be honored with a celebration. The ceremony was meant to appease the bear spirit and to convince it that no harm was done to it by the tribe. The bear meat would be eaten, the bones would be buried, and the skulls were placed in trees.

Among the Ainu people of Japan, the bear is considered the chief of their gods. The Ainu believed that gods would appear to mankind in the form of animals, and that these animals were gifts from the gods meant for eating. In fact, killing and eating the bear released the god from its animal form so it could return to the realm of the gods where it was believed to have a human form. The bears were treated quite well, but were eventually sacrificed – usually in the middle of winter when the bear meat was believed to be at its best with the added winter fat.

The bear is considered a deity in and of itself or is associated with deities and ancestors in a number of ancient cultures including Greece, Russia, Native America, and amid the Celts, Dacians, Thracians, and Getians, in other cultures.

---

seen as one way to conserve semen by transferring it back and forth between men rather than losing it to women through heterosexual sex.

[48] Many native and tribal cultures hold this belief about a variety of animals. Since the animals reincarnate, there is no real harm done by killing and eating them. Often times, if the animals were honored correctly and reverently, they would continue to provide bounty and continue to reincarnate for the tribe's benefit

## Werebears

With the exception of the Norse Berserkers, werebears are usually portrayed as benevolent and protective. This is probably because of the nurturing attributes associated with them as totem animals as well as deeply entrenched mythological associations. In many cultures (such as among the Finns), the bear is worshipped and in others (such as among Native Americans) the bear is seen as a close relative of humans.

## Deities Associated with Bears

**Artemis** – The Greek goddess Artemis has been mentioned previously for her association with wolves, but she also has bear associations and a general reputation for being a protector of wildlife. Priestesses of Artemis included Melissae (honey bees) and Arktoi (bears who love to eat honey). These designations suggest active and passive roles in Lesbian relationships. The Cult of Artemis at Brauron enacted initiation rituals of young girls between the ages of 5 and 10 who "played the bear" for Artemis. The rite itself was called the "arkteia" and the girls imitated she-bears. This rite may have been an initiation of young girls into adolescence, a rite to prepare girls for eventual marriage, or a rite of worship or appeasement to the goddess. Origin myths for the Cult of Artemis at Brauron suggest that it was likely the latter – an appeasement to Artemis for the killing of her sacred stags or bears by hunters. The girls were chosen as representatives from prominent families. They would dedicate themselves to Artemis for a period of time and act out the part of a bear in various rituals to Artemis. In early rituals, they wore actual bear skins, but later they wore saffron robes to represent bear skins when actual bears became scarce in the region. A festival for Artemis was celebrated every four years.[49] Sometimes young boys also participated in these festivals to celebrate Artemis as the Great-she-bear. They too would take on the form of a bear and dance slowly to the tune of a double flute.[50]

**Artio** – Artio is the Celtic Bear Goddess who was worshipped by a Celtic tribe known as the Helvetii. Artio is the goddess of wildlife, harvest, and fertility and she is worshipped as the "she-bear." A statue of Artio was found at Berne[51] in Switzerland. The statue depicts Artio in her human form seated with a bear eating from a bowl of fruit in her lap. The Celts had a male counterpart to Artio named Artaius. The Romans associated Artaius with their own god Mercury.

---

[49] Earlier in history it may have been an annual event.
[50] This type of flute is known as the diaulos.
[51] Meaning "bear".

**Diana** – Diana is the Roman goddess of the hunt, wild animals, the woodlands, the moon, and childbirth. She is strongly associated with virginity and women, and has therefore been adopted as a role model for modern feminists and Lesbians. Modern Dianic Wicca and Witchcraft focus solely on the Goddess - seeing the Goddess as complete unto herself without the need for a male counterpart. Dianic covens are female-exclusive and many Dianic covens exclude those who are not biologically female as determined at birth. Diana, like her Greek counterpart Artemis, is closely related to wolves and bears.

**Callisto and Arcas** – In Greek mythology, Callisto was a nymph and follower of the goddess Artemis. Zeus wanted to have sex with her. Callisto was only interested in Artemis so Zeus transformed himself to look like Artemis and seduced her. The resulting child was named Arcas. Hera became jealous of the union and transformed Callisto into a bear, but Zeus was able to hide Arcas in Arcadia[52] to save him from Hera's wrath[53]. In **Metamorphosis**, Ovid tells an alternate story of King Lycaon's transformation into the first werewolf[54]. In this story, Lycaon tempted Zeus to prove Arcas was his son by burning Arcas on a pyre. Zeus protected Arcas and turned King Lycaon into a werewolf. After this, Arcas became the new king of Arcadia. One day when Arcas was hunting, he came across a she-bear and killed it with an arrow. Unbeknownst to him the bear was actually his mother. Because of this tragedy, Zeus took pity on the two and placed them in the heavens as the constellations – Ursa Major and Ursa Minor[55].

**Nanook** – Nanook is an Inuit Polar Bear god and master of bears. Nanook decided whether hunters would be successful on their hunt and he punished those who violated hunting taboos. Dead bears taken in the hunt would be honored and given offerings. Male bears were given hunting tools and female bears were offered sewing and cooking tools. The Inuit believed that bears wanted to be hunted so that they would be offered tools that they could take with them to the afterlife. If a hunter treated the bears with respect, they would tell their friends who would come to be hunted. If the hunter was disrespectful, the bears would stay away.

---

[52] Arcadia was mentioned in Chapter 2 on Greek Lycanthropes in reference to the story of King Lycaon who was turned into a werewolf by Zeus, and as the home of the festival and initiation rites of Lykaia associated with werewolves.

[53] In other stories it is Artemis (Roman Diana) who transforms Callisto into a bear for breaking her vow of virginity.

[54] I mentioned a different version of King Lycaon's transformation story in Chapter 2 on Greek Lycanthropes.

[55] Translated as the Big Bear and the Little Bear.

**Odin** – The Norse god Odin was already mentioned in Chapter 6 on Norse Werewolves. He is associated with both bears and wolves and with the berserkers and Ulfhednar – bear and wolf warrior bands.

# Chapter 14: Other Man Beasts

## Overview Other Man Beasts

Shapeshifting isn't confined just to the realm of werewolves. A large number of man-beasts exist. These include transformations from human to animal, animal to human, and hybrid human-animal forms.

Shapeshifters and human-animal hybrids are liminal beings. They contain the dual natures of humans and animals. They can be both civilized and wild. They can also express other dual natures such as masculine and feminine. Their animal natures are frequently expressed as lust – either blood lust or sexual lust.

## The story so far

I've talked about Jackal-headed Egyptian gods and the dog-headed Wulvers of Scotland. In the chapter on Roman werewolves, I briefly pointed out a number of transformations into a variety of animals, plants, and other objects as mentioned in Ovid's **Metamorphoses**. I also remarked on how female witches in the Middle Ages were believed to transform into cats and hares. I've mentioned St. Christopher who is often depicted as a cynocephali, a dog-headed man. I'll leave these stories in their respective chapters where you can read them again if you like so I can move forward with other types of animal transformations and hybrids.

## Were-dogs

Wolves are the most popular shapeshifters throughout mythology and folklore. Shapeshifting into dogs comes in a close second, though most people aren't familiar with the technical terms for were-dogs. Cynanthropy is the shapeshifting of a human into a dog and vice-versa. Cynocephali involves a creature with a human body and a dog head.

I have already referenced some cynanthropes and cynocephali in previous chapters, but I will mention a few more instances here.

The Kynokephaloi (also spelled cynocephali) were either an Indian or African tribe of dog-headed men who lived in mountain caves. These tribes are mentioned in several classical accounts including Herodotus' **Histories** and the works of Pliny and Ctesias. They were usually depicted as a kind and just people with the bodies of men and heads of dogs. Their teeth were larger than a dog's and they had animal claws instead of fingernails. They also had tails. They wore animal skins for clothing and communicated by barking, howling and making signs with their hands and fingers. The Kynokephaloi were said to eat raw meat or meat cooked in the sun, and they also raised their own herds and crops

Furthermore, they knew how to make weapons and baskets. Modern scholars believe that these cynocephali mentioned in ancient texts were actually baboons.

In ancient China, four clans of people, known as the Jung, worshipped dogs. They believed the dog was their ancestor. In one legend, a dog wished to marry a princess but her father refused unless he could change into a man. The dog was partially successful gaining the body of a man, but keeping his dog head.

A race of dog-men are depicted in Hawaiian mythology. These dog-men were demigods with mystical powers. They looked like normal men with hairless bodies and the tails of dogs. These dog-men were adept at wrestling and "bone breaking" and some were robbers and cannibals.

## Were-Hyenas

Were-hyenas are common in the folklore in parts of Africa and western Asia. Were-hyenas are often portrayed as hyenas that turn into humans. Humans who transform into hyenas also figure into the folklore.

Early naturalists believed hyenas were hermaphrodites that changed their sex from male to female and then back again. Hyenas were also believed to practice homosexuality. This misconception was due to the female hyena's unique urogenital system. In Arab folklore, hyenas are believed to have the ability to hypnotize victims with their eyes or with their pheromones.

In parts of Africa, blacksmiths are believed to be wizards and witches with the ability to change into hyenas. These "bouda," as they are called, are said to rob graves at midnight. The folklore in the Sudan region suggests a human-hyena hybrid that eats humans and terrorizes lovers. In its human form, this creature is a blacksmith, healer, or woodcutter with excessive hair, red eyes, and a nasal voice.

Among the Korè people of Mali, rituals using masks and role-play as a form of mental shapeshifting are used to scare participants into leading better lives and to avoid the bad habits epitomized in the hyena.

In Persia, people known as the kaftar are said to be human-hyena hybrids that slaughter children.

## Were-cats

The transformation of humans into cats is known as ailuranthropy.

In Africa, were-leopards are often believed to be leopard deities posing as humans. Sometimes they mate with humans producing children that can shapeshift or that have magickal powers. Were-lions are believed to be kings, queens, or other royalty from former lives or those destined for such a position in this life.

In Asia, were-tigers are popular. Indian were-tigers are dark magicians who attack livestock and may even attack and eat humans. Chinese were-tigers may be the result of a hereditary curse or they may be the ghosts of people killed by tigers. To avenge their deaths, these "Chang" encourage tigers to eat more humans. Some of these ghosts could cause humans to turn into man-eating were-tigers. In Thailand, some sorcerers can change into animals; and tigers who eat too many humans might become were-tigers.

Were-tigers in Indonesia and Malaysia are known as the Harimau jadian. These creatures are generally not hostile toward humans unless they have a reason to be. One might become a were-tiger by heredity, spells, charms, fasting, or sheer willpower.

In Japan there is a type of were-cat known as bakeneko, which is similar to the kitsune[56]. Japanese cats are associated with mysterious abilities and are sometimes connected with prostitutes. An elderly cat might become a bakeneko in its later life and might even turn on its owner. Bakeneko are attributed with such abilities as transforming into humans, dancing, human speech, the ability to curse humans, necromancy, the power of possession, and general mischief.

In Mesoamerican cultures, were-jaguars are the norm. This is associated with the religious veneration of the jaguar. Priests and shamans would wear jaguar skins as a form of shapeshifting. Aztec jaguar warriors may have been similar to European wolf warriors and the Norse berserkers. Since pre-Christian Mesoamerican peoples incorporated homosexuality into their culture[57], it is plausible that homosexual initiations may have been involved in the training of Aztec youth to become warriors, including those becoming Jaguar Warriors.

## The Selkie

The Selkie are Scottish shapeshifting seals. Similar creatures are found in Icelandic and Inuit folklore. Both male and female selkies are very beautiful and seductive as humans and wear a seal skin while in their seal form. Male selkie often seduce human women waiting for the return of their fisherman husbands. Human males sometimes steal the seal skins from female selkie forcing them to become their wives. Eventually she finds her seal skin and returns to the sea leaving her human husband and children behind.

## Human – Animal Hybrids

**Satyrs** – Satyrs and fauns are Greek and Roman hybrids with the upper torso of a human and the lower torso of either a goat or a horse. Satyrs are usually male, though female satyrs are known to exist. They are often depicted with goat horns and an erect phallus. They're favorite pastimes are playing the pan pipes; drinking; and chasing after nymphs, maidens, and shepherds. They are often

---

[56] Japanese gender-shifting were-foxes.
[57] Some gods such as Xochipilli presided over homosexuality and male prostitution; male adolescents were given younger boys as sexual partners; and shamans and priests often engaged in homosexuality.

associated with excessive lust and sexual deviancy. They are also associated with the Greek god Dionysus and the Roman god Bacchus.

**Minotaur** – The Minotaur has a human body and the head of a bull. In myth, there was only one Minotaur, though modern fiction often depicts the minotaur as a species. The Minotaur is the result of sexual relations between King Minos of Crete's wife Pasiphae and a bull. According to the story, King Minos failed to sacrifice a snow-white Cretan bull to Poseidon. As a result, Poseidon caused Pasiphae to fall in love with and lust after the bull. She copulated with the bull, became pregnant, and eventually the Minotaur was born. The Minotaur lived in a labyrinth on the island of Crete and devoured humans sent into the maze as tributes. Ultimately, the Minotaur was killed by the hero Theseus who was aided by King Minos' daughter Ariadne.

**Centaur** – Centaurs have the body of a horse and the upper torso of a human. Unlike satyrs which also sometimes have the lower body of a horse, Centaurs have all four legs of a horse as well as human arms whereas Satyrs had only the rear legs and thighs. Most centaurs are depicted as lustful and wild. Centaurs are generally male, though female centaurs, called Kentaurides, are sometimes mentioned.

One of the most famous centaurs is Chiron who is known for his role as a healer and as a teacher. Chiron was different from other centaurs in that he was more civilized and frequently depicted with human forelegs. Chiron was a tutor and erastes[58] to numerous Greek characters including Achilles, Aesculapius, Jason (of the Argonauts), Ajax, Aeneas, Actaeon, Caeneus, Theseus, Telamon, Peleus, Aristaios, and others.

**Harpy** – Harpies are hybrid creatures with the body and wings of a bird and the face and sometimes upper torso (breasts included) of a woman. Earlier depictions show them as beautiful women with wings and later depictions show them as hideous monsters. Either way, they are vicious and cruel. Harpies are frequently associated with the wind and their favorite pastime is stealing food from people. They're second favorite pastime is abducting and torturing evildoers. The often deliver wrongdoers to either the Furies or to Tartarus for punishment.

**Nagas** – Nagas are human-snake hybrids and shapeshifters found in Hinduism, Buddhism, Jainism, and Sikhism. A Naga can be male or female[59]. Nagas are frequently seen as deities or supernatural creatures separate from humans. They may be malevolent, benevolent, or neutral beings depending on the story. A Naga might be depicted as a human from the waist up and a snake from the

---

[58] Older male in Greek homosexual apprentice relationships.
[59] Female Nagas are called Nagi or Nagini.

waist down. It could also be an extremely large snake, often a king cobra. Some Nagas are snakes that take on a human form. Nagas are frequently seen as nature spirits that protect springs, rivers, and other bodies of water. They also bring rain, fertility, and prosperity, and are believed to hold the secret to immortality.

The serpent is an obvious phallic symbol. Snake worship and phallic worship often go hand in hand. The snake is frequently seen as a symbol of fertility because of its similarity to a phallus. Snakes are also associated with healing, regeneration, rebirth, and even immortality because of the way they shed their skin on a regular basis.

Some deities and religious figures are associated with Nagas and other serpents. These include Vishnu, Ganesha, Shiva, and the Buddha.

One Buddhist story depicts a homosexual relationship (or at least a strong bromance) between a Naga and an ascetic. In the story known as the Manikantha Jataka, a Naga king named Manikantha while in human form meets and befriends an unnamed ascetic. They become very close and the Naga sheds his human form and lies with the man taking him into his folds and covering him with his hood[60]. The ascetic is greatly afraid of the Naga in snake form and becomes sickly and pale. The Naga wears a sacred jewel around his throat and to discourage the snake from visiting him again the ascetic begs Manikantha for the jewel. The Naga is insulted and refuses to see the ascetic again. The ascetic continues to grow sickly and weak, only now it's because he can no longer live without his lover and friend. The moral of the story is not to beg from friends.

## Mermaids / Mermen

Mermaids are hybrid creatures with the lower body of a fish and the upper body of a woman. Mermen are the male versions of these creatures with the upper body of a man. Both Mermaids and Mermen can be benevolent or malevolent toward humans. They might summon storms to sink ships or lure humans to their deaths, but they might also fall in love with humans, protect them while sailing, or bestow gifts to them. They are also said to have magickal abilities such as brewing potions, lifting curses, and curing illnesses. Mermen are sometimes portrayed as teachers.

Mermen might be ugly with seaweed hair, pointy teeth, and other deformities or they might be beautiful men like their female counterparts.

Closely related to mermaids and mermen are the Nereids, a tribe of sea-nymphs in Greek mythology. The Nereids have shapeshifting powers and were often worshipped in ancient Greek port cities and by fishermen and sailors. Nereids appear to have Lesbian associations preferring each other's company to that of men or even mermen. They are also associated with male couples such as Achilles and Patroclus whose deaths they mourned.

---

[60] "Taking him into his folds" is possibly a metaphor for sexuality and perhaps the "hood" is his foreskin - just an educated guess on my part.

**One interesting side note related to mermaids in literature rather than in mythology and folklore:**

Hans Christian Anderson's fairytale about the "Little Mermaid" was likely influenced by his own homosexuality and his relationship with a young man named Edvard Collin. In the original tale, a mermaid is rescued by a prince and falls in love with him. She makes a deal with a sea-witch to become human, but in her human form she cannot speak. The sea-witch also warns her that if the mermaid doesn't earn the prince's love then she will die of a broken heart. The prince is in an arranged marriage and although the prince cares for the mermaid, he ultimately goes through with the wedding. The mermaid dies and becomes an ethereal being. The story is an allusion to Anderson's tragic love for Collin who eventually marries a woman.

## <u>Final Thoughts</u>

Were-creatures and animal-human hybrids take on a variety of forms in cultures around the world and throughout history. They take the forms of mammals, birds, fish, reptiles, amphibians, and even insects. It is beyond the scope of this book to list all of them or all the stories, myths, and folklore that surround them.

# Conclusion

Werewolves, were-creatures, and animal human hybrids are intimately connected to homosexuality in the history, mythology, and folklore of many cultures. This connection includes homosexual initiations into religious-warrior cults, homosexual coming of age rites, associations with gender-variant deities and heroes, and werewolves and shapeshifters who were or were thought to have homosexual lovers.

The werewolf often serves as a metaphor for homosexuality as both werewolves and those of homosexual, bisexual, or transgender nature exist as liminal creatures somewhere at the outskirts of society. Here they exist in a state somewhere between the arbitrary norms of society – whether this be between man and beast, male and female, heterosexual and homosexual, tame and wild, and acceptable and unacceptable. In some cultures shapeshifting and homosexuality are considered in a positive light, where they serve a constructive function to society. In others, they are seen as deviant, as dangerous, and as something to be controlled or wiped out.

Closely related are practices involving shamanism which often includes shapeshifting, gender-shifting, astral travel in animal form, and the deconstruction and transformation of self. In fact, in a number of cultures sexual or gender variance was a pre-requisite for many to become shamans, magicians, healers, and medicine men whether serving alone or in societies, bands, and cults with others.

Modern LGBT folks can find meaning in the old werewolf and shapeshifter stories, myths, and archetypes; and they can also ascribe their own meanings as archetypes and myths are ageless, timeless, and continually reinterpreted.

The next book in this series, will focus on modern werewolf and shapeshifter mythology as seen through the lens of movies, television, fiction writing, music, and pop culture. As with this book, wherever possible links between werewolves and LGBT folks will be made.

## For Further Reading:

*All websites were accessed during the years 2014 – 2016.*

## Chapter 1

Buddy. I Love Werewolves, "Identifying a werewolf in human form": http://ilovewerewolves.com/identifying-a-werewolf-in-human-form/

Senn, Harry. "Romanian Werewolves: Seasons, Ritual, Cycles": **Folklore**, Vol. 93, No. 2. 1982. P. 206-215.

Wikipedia, "Beast of Gévaudan": http://en.wikipedia.org/wiki/Beast_of_G%C3%A9vauda n

Wikipedia, "Shapeshifting": http://en.wikipedia.org/wiki/List_of_shapeshifters_i n_myth_and_fiction

Wikipedia, "Silver Bullet": http://en.wikipedia.org/wiki/Silver_bullet

Wikipedia, "Therianthropy": http://en.wikipedia.org/wiki/Therianthropy

Wikipedia, "Werewolf": http://en.wikipedia.org/wiki/Lycanthropy

## Chapter 2

Herodotus. **Histories**, "Book Four", c. 440 BC

Irving, P. M. C. Forbes. **Metamorphosis in Greek Myths.** Clarendon Press. Oxford. 1990.

Kunstler, Barton. "The Werewolf Figure and Its Adoption into the Greek Political Volcabulary": The Classical World, Vol. 84, No. 3. Jan. – Feb. 1991. p. 1989-2005.

Plato. **The Republic**, "Book VIII", c. 380 BC.

Sergent, Bernard. **Homosexuality in Greek Myth**. Beacon Press, Boston. 1984.

Theoi Greek Mythology, "Leto": http://www.theoi.com/Titan/TitanisLeto.html

Wikipedia, "Artemis": http://en.wikipedia.org/wiki/Artemis

Wikipedia, "Homosexuality in ancient Greece": http://en.wikipedia.org/wiki/Homosexuality_in_ancient_Greece

Wikipedia, "Leto": http://en.wikipedia.org/wiki/Leto

Wikipedia, "Lyceus": https://en.wikipedia.org/wiki/Lyceus

Wikipedia, "Lykaia": http://en.wikipedia.org/wiki/Lykaia

Wikipedia, "Neuri": http://en.wikipedia.org/wiki/Neuri

Wikipedia, "Vrykolakas": http://en.wikipedia.org/wiki/Vrykolakas

Wolves and Humans Foundation, "Origins of a Myth – The Wolves of Greece": http://www.wolvesandhumans.org/pdf-documents/Wolves%20in%20Greece%20article.pdf

## Chapter 3

About.com, "Sections from *The Satyricon* of Petronius Arbiter – 'The Dinner of Trimalchio": http://ancienthistory.about.com/library/bl/bl_text_satyricon2_ghoststory.htm

Greenberg, David. **The Construction of Homosexuality**. The University of Chicago Press. Chicago. 1990.

Muse, Frank. Queer Gods for Queer Men Blog. "A Brief History of Gay Werewolves: Part 1, the Ancient World": http://queergodsforqueermen.blogspot.com/2011/10/brief-history-of-gay-werewolves-part-1.html : October 1, 2011.

Neill, James. **The Origins and Role of Same-Sex Relations in Human Societies.** McFarland & Company, Inc., North Carolina. 2009.

The Pagan Library. "Lupercalia: She-
Wolf": http://www.paganlibrary.com/reference/lupercalia.php

Poetry in Translation. Virgil. **The
Eclogues**. http://www.poetryintranslation.com/PITBR/Latin/Virgi
lEclogues.htm

Rayne. She Wolf Night Blog. http://she-wolf-
night.blogspot.com/2011/02/wolf-goddess-luperca.html : February
14, 2011.

Roman Myth Index, "Luperca": http://mythindex.com/roman-
mythology/L/Luperca.html

Secundus, C. Plinius. **The Eigth Booke of Historie of Natvre.** Translated by
Philemon Holland.
1601. http://penelope.uchicago.edu/holland/pliny8.html

Wikipedia, "Diana
(mythology)": http://en.wikipedia.org/wiki/Diana_(mythology)

Wikipedia, "Hermaphroditus": http://en.wikipedia.org/wiki/Hermaphroditus

Wikipedia, "List of *Metamorphoses*
characters": http://en.wikipedia.org/wiki/List_of_Metamorphoses_c
haracters

Wikipedia, "Lupercalia": http://en.wikipedia.org/wiki/Lupercalia

Wikipedia, "Satyricon": http://en.wikipedia.org/wiki/Satyricon

Wikipedia, "Werewolf": http://en.wikipedia.org/wiki/Werewolf

Wikipedia for Schools, "Hyena": http://schools-
wikipedia.org/wp/h/Hyena.htm

## Chapter 4

Dybas, Sheryl Lyn. Natural History. "Return of the Wolf
God": http://www.naturalhistorymag.com/features/032450/return-
of-the-wolf-god

Moonlight. Werewolves.com.
"Wepwawet": http://www.werewolves.com/wepwawet/ : August 7,
2010.

Wikipedia, "Egyptian Wolf": http://en.wikipedia.org/wiki/Egyptian_Wolf

Wikipedia, "Imiut fetish": http://en.wikipedia.org/wiki/Imiut_fetish

Wikipedia, "Lycopolis": http://en.wikipedia.org/wiki/Lycopolis

Wikipedia, Wepwawet: http://en.wikipedia.org/wiki/Wepwawet

Your Lupine Life, "Egyptian
Werewolves": http://yourlupinelife.com/egyptian-werewolves

## Chapter 5

About.com: About Religion & Spirituality: Paganism / Wicca, "Cailleach, the
Ruler of
Winter": http://paganwiccan.about.com/od/celticdeities/p/Cailleach
Profil.htm

Bard Mythologies, "Cormac Mac Art": http://bardmythologies.com/cormac-
mac-art/

Celtic Literature Collective & Jones's Celtic Encyclopedia, "The History of
Taliesin": http://www.maryjones.us/ctexts/taliesin.html

Conner, Randy P., Hatfield, David, et al. **Cassell's Encyclopedia of Queer
Myth, Symbol, and Spirit**. London. 1997.

Doc Conjure. The Demoniacal,
"Faoladh": http://thedemoniacal.blogspot.com/2011/12/faoladh.htm
l : December 22, 2011.

Fuller, David Jon. As You Were (A.K.A. Official Website of David Jon Fuller),
"Interview: Dr. Phillip Bernhardt-House on Celtic
Werewolves": http://www.davidjonfuller.com/2012/10/17/interview
-dr-phillip-bernhardt-house-on-celtic-werewolves/ : October 17, 2012.

Hine, Phil. Philhine.org.uk, "Bums in Brigantia: Sacred Gender-Variance in Ancient Germanic & Celtic Cultures": http://www.philhine.org.uk/writings/flsh_bumsb.html

Hostina, Nashoba. Lycanthropy, Werewolfery, and Lycanthropy: Self-Medicating with Werewolves, "Faoladh": http://lycantherapy.tumblr.com/post/34883563577/faoladh-while-theyre-no-longer-there-ireland-was

Hub Pages: Religion and Philosophy: Paganism & Witchcraft, "The Wolf – Ancestral Guardian & Power Spirit": http://hubpages.com/hub/Call-Of-The-Wild-The-Wolf-In-Mythology-Power-Animal : Feburary 5, 2015.

Luminarium, "Cormac Mac Art": http://www.luminarium.org/mythology/ireland/cormac.htm

Luminarium, "The Birth of Cormac Mac Art": http://www.luminarium.org/mythology/ireland/cormacbirth.htm

McColman. **The Complete Idiot's Guide to Celtic Wisdom**. Alpha Books, New York. 2003.

Moonlight. Werewolves.com, "Legendary Irish Wolf Warriors": http://www.werewolves.com/legendary-irish-wolf-warriors/ : April 26, 2011.

Niafer, Fenian. Ancient Worlds: Celtia, "Faoladh (Werewolf): http://www.ancientworlds.net/aw/Article/1203825

Pagans Circle, "Cormac mac Airt": http://www.paganscircle.org/cormac-mac-airt

Sinn, Shanon. Living Library, "The Celtic Werewolf": http://livinglibraryblog.com/?p=656 : April 18, 2012.

Squire, Charles. Sacred Texts, **Celtic Myth and Legend**, "Chapter IV: The Religion of the Ancient Britons and Druidism"" http://www.sacred-texts.com/neu/celt/cml/cml08.htm#page_40 : (1905).

Summers, Montague. **The Werewolf.** University Books, New York. 1966.

Tam B. Histories of Things to Come, "All Hallows' Eve Countdown: Heroic
    Werewolves: http://historiesofthingstocome.blogspot.com/2013/10/
    all-hallows-eve-countdown-heroic.html : October 9, 2013.

Timeless Myths: Celtic Mythology,
    "Mabinogion": http://www.timelessmyths.com/celtic/mabinogion.ht
    ml

Salmon, John. "Druidical Sacrifices in Ireland: Were there human victims?",
    **Ulster Journal of Archaeology**, Volume 1, Belfast. 1895. p. 218-226.

Werewolf Wiki, "B. Werewolf legends in Western Europe, Continental and
    Insular": https://werewolfwiki.wikispaces.com/B.++Werewolf+legen
    ds+in+Western+Europe%2C+Continental+and+Insular

Wikipedia, "Airitech": http://en.wikipedia.org/wiki/Airitech

Wikipedia, "Cailleach": http://en.wikipedia.org/wiki/Cailleach

Wikipedia, "Cernunnos": http://en.wikipedia.org/wiki/Cernunnos

Wikipedia (de), "Cóir
    Anmann": http://de.wikipedia.org/wiki/C%C3%B3ir_Anmann

Wikipedia, "Cormac mac
    Airt": http://en.wikipedia.org/wiki/Cormac_mac_Airt

Wikipedia, "Crom Cruach": http://en.wikipedia.org/wiki/Crom_Cruach

Wikipedia, "Tuatha Dé
    Danann": http://en.wikipedia.org/wiki/Tuatha_D%C3%A9_Danann

Wikipedia, "Wolves in
    Ireland": http://en.wikipedia.org/wiki/Wolves_in_Ireland

## Chapter 6

Clark, Alisdair. Aryan Futurism, "Mannerbund and
    Homosexuality": http://aryanfuturism.blogspot.com/2006/03/manne
    rbund-and-homosexuality.html : March 28, 2006.

Greenberg, David. **The Construction of Homosexuality**. The University of Chicago Press. Chicago. 1990.

Guðmundsdóttir, Aðalheiður. University of Iceland. "The Werewolf in Medieval Icelandic Literature", **The Journal of English and Germanic Philology**, Vol. 106, No. 3, July 2007.

Hine, Phil. Philhine.org.uk, "Bums in Brigantia: Sacred Gender-Variance in Ancient Germanic & Celtic Cultures": http://www.philhine.org.uk/writings/flsh_bumsb.html

McCoy, Dan. Norse Mythology for Smart People, "Skadi": http://norse-mythology.org/gods-and-creatures/giants/skadi/

McCoy, Dan. Norse Mythology for Smart People, "Skoll and Hati": http://norse-mythology.org/skoll-hati/

Mamtc. Myths and Mythology – The Commons, "Wolves-Hati and Skoll and Serpent-Rahu and Kethu – Eclipse Story": http://mamtc.blogspot.com/2011/08/wolves-hati-and-skoll-and-serpent-rahu.html : August 25, 2011.

Stereoagnostic. Mythical Creatures Guide, "Fenris Wolf: http://www.mythicalcreaturesguide.com/page/Fenris+Wolf : July 18, 2010.

Vanggaard, Thorkil. **Phallos: A Symbol and Its History in the Male World**. International Universities Press. New York, 1974.

Wikipedia, "Berserker": http://en.wikipedia.org/wiki/Berserker

Wikipedia, "Ergi": http://en.wikipedia.org/wiki/Ergi

Wikipedia, "Fenris": http://en.wikipedia.org/wiki/Fenris

Wikipedia, "Geri and Freki": http://en.wikipedia.org/wiki/Geri_and_Freki

Wikipedia, "Hati Hróðvitnisson": http://en.wikipedia.org/wiki/Hati_Hr%C3%B3%C3%B0vitnisson

Wikipedia, "Járnviðr": http://en.wikipedia.org/wiki/J%C3%A1rnvi%C3%B0r

Wikipedia, "Loki": http://en.wikipedia.org/wiki/Loki

Wikipedia, "Sköll": http://en.wikipedia.org/wiki/Sk%C3%B6ll

## Chapter 7

Rowlands, Alison. **Witchcraft and Masculinities in Early Modern Europe.** Palgrave McMillan, New York. 2009.

Schulte, Rolf. **Man as Witch: Male Witches in Central Europe**. Palgrave McMillan, New York. 2009.

Summers, Montague. **The Werewolf.** University Books, New York. 1966.

Wikipedia, "Buggery Act 1533": http://en.wikipedia.org/wiki/Buggery_Act_1533

Wikipedia, "Familiar Spirit": http://en.wikipedia.org/wiki/Familiar_spirit

Wikipedia, "Flying Ointment": https://en.wikipedia.org/wiki/Flying_ointment

Wikipedia, "Peter Stumpp": https://en.wikipedia.org/wiki/Peter_Stumpp

Wikipedia, "Sodomy": http://en.wikipedia.org/wiki/Sodomy

Wikipedia, "Werewolf witch trials": http://en.wikipedia.org/wiki/Werewolf_witch_trials

Wikipedia, "Wolfssegen": http://en.wikipedia.org/wiki/Wolfssegen

## Chapter 8

1onewolf.com, "Wolf Legend and Lore": http://1onewolf.com/lakota/Wolf/folklore.htm

Beacom, Betsy. eHow, "Shape Shifters in Native American Myths": http://www.ehow.com/info_8625863_indian-legends-wolf.html

Boswell, John. **Same-Sex Unions in Pre-modern Europe**. Vintage Books, New York. 1995.

Donovan, Jack and Nathan F. Miller. **Blood Brotherhood and Other Rites of Male Alliance**. Published by Jack Donovan, Portland, Oregon, 2009.

Encyclopaedia Britannica, "Coyote: Mythology": http://www.britannica.com/EBchecked/topic/141380/Coyote

Gods and Monsters.com, "History of the Werewolf": http://www.gods-and-monsters.com/history-of-the-werewolf.html : Royal Mint Publishing, LLC.

Kgontarc. Trans Bodies Across the Globe: Department of Gender Studies, Indiana University Bloomington, "Navajo Cultural Constructions of Gender and Sexuality": https://transgenderglobe.wordpress.com/2010/12/17/navajo-cultural-constructions-of-gender-and-sexuality/: December 17, 2010.

Moonlight. Werewolves.com, "Native American Wolf Gods": http://www.werewolves.com/native-american-wolf-gods/: July 8, 2010.

Native-languages.org, "Legendary Native American Figures: Chibiabos (Jiibayaabooz)": http://www.native-languages.org/chibiabos.htm

Native-languages.org, "Native American Wolf Mythology": http://www.native-languages.org/legends-wolf.htm

Thomas, Welsey. **Two-Spirit People**, "Navajo Cultural Constructions of Gender and Sexuality". University of Illinois Press, Urbana-Champaign. 1997.

Warpaths2peacepipes.com, "Animism & Animists": http://www.warpaths2peacepipes.com/native-american-culture/animism.htm

Wikipedia, "Animism": http://en.wikipedia.org/wiki/Animism

Wikipedia, "Coyote (mythology): http://en.wikipedia.org/wiki/Coyote_(mythology)

Wikipedia, "Coyote (Navajo mythology)": http://en.wikipedia.org/wiki/Coyote_(Navajo_mythology)

Wikipedia, "Glooscap": http://en.wikipedia.org/wiki/Glooscap

Wikipedia, "Malsumis": http://en.wikipedia.org/wiki/Malsumis

Wikipedia, "Nagual": http://en.wikipedia.org/wiki/Nagual

Wikipedia, "Skin Walker": http://en.wikipedia.org/wiki/Skin-walker

Wikipedia, "Trickster": http://en.wikipedia.org/wiki/Trickster

Wikipedia, "Wolves in folklore, religion, and mythology: http://en.wikipedia.org/wiki/Wolves_in_folklore,_religion_and_mythology

## Chapter 9

Brown, Nathan. **The Complete Idiot's Guide to Werewolves.** Alpha Books, New York. 2009.

Hamel, Frank. **Werewolves, Bird-Women, Tiger-Men and Other Human Animals**. Dover Publications, Inc., Mineola, New York. 2007.

Karg, Barb. **The Girl's Guide to Werewolves: All You Need to Know about the Original Untamed Bad Boys**. Adams Media, Avon, Massachusetts, 2009.

Sconduto, Leslie. **Metamorphosis of the Werewolf**. McFarland & Company, Inc., Jefferson, N.C. 2008.

Wikipedia, "Ailbe of Emly": http://en.wikipedia.org/wiki/Ailbe_of_Emly

Wikipedia, "Canon Episcopi": https://en.wikipedia.org/wiki/Canon_Episcopi

Wikipedia, "City of God (book)": http://en.wikipedia.org/wiki/City_of_God_(book)

Wikipedia, "Hubertus": http://en.wikipedia.org/wiki/Hubertus

Wikipedia, "Maleus
    Maleficarum": http://en.wikipedia.org/wiki/Malleus_Maleficarum

Wikipedia, "Saint Hubert's
    Key": http://en.wikipedia.org/wiki/Saint_Hubert%27s_Key

Wikipedia,
    "Transubstantiation": http://en.wikipedia.org/wiki/Transubstantiatio
    n

Wikipedia, "Wolves in folklore, religion, and
    mythology": http://en.wikipedia.org/wiki/Wolves_in_folklore,_religi
    on_and_mythology

## **Chapter 10**

Cochrane, Ev. The Book of Persephone (Things in Three) Blog. "Apollo
    (Greek God Apollo
    Reconsidered)": http://thingsinthree.blogspot.com/p/greek-god-
    apollo-reconsidered-by-ev.html

Blutwolfin (fenriSS), White Pride Worldwide[61], "History of the
    Heruli": https://www.stormfront.org/forum/t208255/ : May 30,
    2005.

Donlan, Gershenson, Daniel E. "Review of **Apollo the Wolf-God** by Daniel
    E. Gershenson": **The Classical World**. Vol. 87. No. 4. Mar.-Apr.
    1994. p. 321-322.

Gill, N.S. About Education. "The Role and Performance of the Luperci at the
    Lupercalia": http://ancienthistory.about.com/od/socialcustomsdailylif
    e/a/010908Lupercal_3.htm : October 23, 2015.

---

[61]     I personally do not support white separatist, nationalist, or supremacist
organizations or viewpoints. However they do seem to have a huge interest in and
knowledge of European history and mythology. The information presented in this post seems
to be historically accurate and not particularly offensive, racist, or homophobic. This post
mentions ritual homosexuality among the Heruli, so I did use some of this information in
chapter 10. Rather than censoring or covering up this source, I've chosen to list it - be that as
it may.

Greenberg, David. **The Construction of Homosexuality**. The University of Chicago Press. Chicago. 1990.

Hine, Phil. Philhine.org.uk, "Bums in Brigantia: Sacred Gender-Variance in Ancient Germanic & Celtic Cultures": http://www.philhine.org.uk/writings/flsh_bumsb.html

Kershaw, Kris. "The One-eyed God: Odin and the (Indo-)Germanic Mannerbunde". **Journal of Indo-European Studies Monograph No. 36.** Institute for the Study of Man, Inc. Washington D.C. 2000.

Morison, William. "The Lyceum". Internet Encyclopedia of Philosophy: A Peer-Reviewed Academic Resource: http://www.iep.utm.edu/lyceum/

Neill, James. **The Origins and Role of Same-Sex Relations in Human Societies.** McFarland & Company, Inc., North Carolina. 2009.

Powell, Eric A. "Wolf Rites of Winter". **Archaelogy: A publication of the Archaeological Institute of America**, September 17, 2013: http://www.archaeology.org/issues/102-1309/features/1205-timber-grave-culture-krasnosamarskoe-bronze-age

Rissanen, Mika. "The Hirpi Sorani and the Wolf Cults of Central Italy". **Actos: Acta Philologica Fennica**, Vol. XLVI. 2012. P. 115-35: https://www.academia.edu/2177407/The_Hirpi_Sorani_and_the_Wolf_Cults_of_Central_Italy

Roman Myth Index, "Feronia": http://www.mythindex.com/roman-mythology/F/Feronia.html

Roman Myth Index, "Soranus": http://www.mythindex.com/roman-mythology/S/Soranus.html

Silva, Francisco Vas da. "Sexual Horns: The Anatomy and Metaphysics of Cuckoldry in European Folklore": **Comparative Studies in Society and History**, Vol. 48, No. 2. April 2006. P. 396-418.

Steiger, Brad. **The Werewolf Book: The Encyclopedia of Shape-Shifting Beings.** Visible Ink Press, Canton, MI. 2012.

Wikipedia, "Apellai": https://en.wikipedia.org/wiki/Apellai

Wikipedia, "Danaus": https://en.wikipedia.org/wiki/Danaus

Wikipedia, "Heruli": https://en.wikipedia.org/wiki/Heruli

Wikipedia, "Lupercalia": https://en.wikipedia.org/wiki/Lupercalia

Wikipedia, "Procopius": https://en.wikipedia.org/wiki/Procopius

Wikipedia, "Soranus
(mythology)": https://en.wikipedia.org/wiki/Soranus_(mythology)

Wolf Warriors: http://www.angelfire.com/realm/vlachs/

## Chapter 11

Baird, Jonathan David. NukeMars.com, "Seductive Beasts: The Female
Werewolf in Victorian Literature": http://nukemars.com/?p=1828 :
November 12, 2012.

Bibliophilopolis, "The White Wolf of the Hartz Mountains by Frederick
Marryat": https://bibliophilica.wordpress.com/2014/04/12/the-
white-wolf-of-the-hartz-mountains-by-frederick-marryat/ : April 12,
2014.

Housman, Clemence. Project Gutenberg, "The Werewolf by Clemence
Housman": http://www.gutenberg.org/files/13131/13131-h/13131-
h.htm : August 7, 2004.

Marryat, Frederick. Project Gutenberg, "The White Wolf and More by
Frederick
Marryat": http://gutenberg.net.au/ebooks06/0606061h.html : August
2006.

Moore, C. L. **Werewoman**. 1938.

Saki. Eastoftheweb short stories, "Saki: The She
Wolf": http://www.eastoftheweb.com/short-
stories/UBooks/SheWolf.shtml

Thomas, G.W. Rage Machine Books, "'The Werewolf' (1896) by Clemence
Houseman": http://www.gwthomas.org/houseman.htm

Wikipedia, "Acacallis
    (mythology)": http://en.wikipedia.org/wiki/Acacallis_(mythology)

Wikipedia, "Atalanta": http://en.wikipedia.org/wiki/Atalanta

Wikipedia, "Miletus": http://en.wikipedia.org/wiki/Miletus_(mythology)

Wikipedia, "Shapeshifting": http://en.wikipedia.org/wiki/Shapeshifting

Wikipedia, "Werewoman": http://en.wikipedia.org/wiki/Werewoman

Wratislaw, A. H. Sacred Texts. **Sixty Folk-Tales from Exclusively Slavonic
    Sources.** "LV.—The She-Wolf": http://www.sacred-
    texts.com/neu/sfs/sfs72.htm : (1890).

## Chapter 12

Conner, Randy P., Hatfield, David, et al. **Cassell's Encyclopedia of Queer
    Myth, Symbol, and Spirit**. London. 1997.

GreekMythology.com,
    "Dionysus": http://www.greekmythology.com/Other_Gods/Dionysu
    s/dionysus.html

Penczak, Christopher. **Gay Witchcraft: Empowering the Tribe**. Red Wheel
    / Weiser, LLC., York Beach, ME. 2003.

Theoi Greek Mythology,
    "Dionysus": http://www.theoi.com/Olympios/Dionysos.html

Wikipedia, "Aphroditus": http://en.wikipedia.org/wiki/Aphroditus

Wikipedia, "Dionysus": http://en.wikipedia.org/wiki/Dionysus

Wikipedia, "Ganesha": http://en.wikipedia.org/wiki/Ganesha

Wikipedia, "Hermaphroditus": http://en.wikipedia.org/wiki/Hermaphroditus

Wikipedia, "Hieros gamos": http://en.wikipedia.org/wiki/Hieros_gamos

Wikipedia, "Inari Ōkami": http://en.wikipedia.org/wiki/Inari_%C5%8Ckami

Wikipedia, "Kitsune": http://en.wikipedia.org/wiki/Kitsune

Wikipedia, "LGBT themes in
mythology": http://en.wikipedia.org/wiki/LGBT_themes_in_mythology

Wikipedia, "List of shapeshifters in myth and
fiction": http://en.wikipedia.org/wiki/List_of_shapeshifters_in_myth_and_fiction

Wikipedia, "Transgenderism and
religion": http://en.wikipedia.org/wiki/Transgenderism_and_religion

## Chapter 13

Advocate.com Editors, The Advocate, "#TBT: When *The Advocate* Invented
Bears": http://www.advocate.com/comedy/2014/04/17/tbt-when-advocate-invented-bears : April 17, 2014.

Conner, Randy P., Hatfield, David, et al. **Cassell's Encyclopedia of Queer
Myth, Symbol, and Spirit**. London. 1997.

Dodd, David B. and Christopher A. Faraone. **Initiation in Ancient Greek
Rituals and Narratives**. Routledge, New York, 2003.

Get Bear Smart Society, "About Bears: Food and
Diet": http://www.bearsmart.com/about-bears/food-diet/

Hyena, Hank. Gettingit.com: a webzine, "Semen Warriors of New Guinea: For
them 'gays in the military' is a
necessity: http://www.gettingit.com/article/56 : September 16, 1999.

Journeying to the Goddess, "Goddess
Artio": https://journeyingtothegoddess.wordpress.com/2012/02/03/goddess-artio/ : February 3, 2012.

Legg, David. The Order of Bards Ovates & Druids, "The
Bear": http://www.druidry.org/library/animals/bear

Moonlight. Werewolves.com, "The Werewolf's Cousin: The
Werebear": http://www.werewolves.com/the-werewolf%E2%80%99s-cousin-the-werebear/ : December 3, 2010.

Myth Encyclopedia: Myths and Legends of the World, "Diana": http://www.mythencyclopedia.com/Cr-Dr/Diana.html

Tremblay, PJ. The Gay / Bisexual Male Suicidality Home Page, "Semen 'Cults': Melanesia": http://www.youth-suicide.com/gay-bisexual/semen/10-semen-cults-melenesia.htm

Walker, Wave (Donna). Goddess School: Ancient Mystery School and Teachings with GrannyMoon, "Artio: Celtic Bear Goddess": http://goddessschool.com/projects/wavewalker/11fpartio.html : June 2009.

Wikipedia, "Arcas": http://en.wikipedia.org/wiki/Arcas

Wikipedia, "Bear Worship": http://en.wikipedia.org/wiki/Bear_worship

Wikipedia, "Bear (gay culture): http://en.wikipedia.org/wiki/Bear_(gay_culture)

Wikipedia, "Callisto (mythology): http://en.wikipedia.org/wiki/Callisto_(mythology)

Wikipedia, "Cult of Artemis at Brauron": http://en.wikipedia.org/wiki/Cult_of_Artemis_at_Brauron

Wikipedia, "Diana (mythology)": http://en.wikipedia.org/wiki/Diana_(mythology)

Wikipedia, "Dianic Wicca": http://en.wikipedia.org/wiki/Dianic_Wicca

Wikipedia, "Nanook": http://en.wikipedia.org/wiki/Nanook

## Chapter 14

Buddy. I Love Werewolves, "Cynanthropy or Weredogs": http://ilovewerewolves.com/cynanthropy-weredogs/ : December 10, 2012

Conner, Randy P., Hatfield, David, et al. **Cassell's Encyclopedia of Queer Myth, Symbol, and Spirit**. London. 1997.

GreekMythology.com,
  "Centaur": http://www.greekmythology.com/Myths/Creatures/Centaur/centaur.html

Neill, James. **The Origins and Role of Same-Sex Relations in Human Societies.** McFarland & Company, Inc., North Carolina. 2009.

Norton, Rictor. Gay History & Literature, "A Fairy Tale: The Gay Love Letters of Hans Christian Andersen": http://rictornorton.co.uk/andersen.htm : 1998

Rowlands, Alison. **Witchcraft and Masculinities in Early Modern Europe.** Palgrave McMillan, New York. 2009.

Theoi Greek Mythology,
  "Kynokephaloi": http://www.theoi.com/Phylos/Kunokephaloi.html

Theoi Greek Mythology,
  "Kheiron": http://www.theoi.com/Georgikos/KentaurosKheiron.html

Faithology.com, "Homosexuality in Buddhism": http://www.faithology.com/topics/homosexuality-in-buddhism

Varner, Gary R. **Creatures in the Mist: Little People, Wild Men and Spirit Beings Around the World**. Algora Publishing, New York. 2007.

White, David Gordon. **Myths of the Dog-Man**. University of Chicago Press, Chicago. 1991.

Wikipedia, "Bakeneko": http://en.wikipedia.org/wiki/Bakeneko

Wikipedia, "Centaur": http://en.wikipedia.org/wiki/Centaur

Wikipedia, "Cynanthropy": http://en.wikipedia.org/wiki/Cynanthropy

Wikipedia, "Cynocephaly": http://en.wikipedia.org/wiki/Cynocephaly

Wikipedia, "Harpy": http://en.wikipedia.org/wiki/Harpy

Wikipedia, "Jaguar Warrior": http://en.wikipedia.org/wiki/Jaguar_warrior

Wikipedia, "LGBT history in
    Mexico": http://en.wikipedia.org/wiki/LGBT_history_in_Mexico

Wikipedia, "List of hybrid creatures in
    mythology": http://en.wikipedia.org/wiki/List_of_hybrid_creatures_i
    n_mythology

Wikipedia, "List of Shapeshifters in myth and
    fiction": http://en.wikipedia.org/wiki/List_of_shapeshifters_in_myth
    _and_fiction

Wikipedia, "Mermaid": http://en.wikipedia.org/wiki/Mermaid

Wikipedia, "Merman": http://en.wikipedia.org/wiki/Merman

Wikipedia, "Nāga": http://en.wikipedia.org/wiki/N%C4%81ga

Wikipedia, "Satyr": http://en.wikipedia.org/wiki/Satyr

Wikipedia, "Therianthropy": http://en.wikipedia.org/wiki/Therianthropy

Wikipedia, "Werecat": https://en.wikipedia.org/wiki/Werecat

Wikipedia, "Werehyena": http://en.wikipedia.org/wiki/Werehyena

Wikipedia for Schools, "Hyena": http://schools-
    wikipedia.org/wp/h/Hyena.htm

## General

Copper, Basil. **The Werewolf: In Legend, Fact & Art**. St. Martin's Press,
    New York and London. 1977.

Feher-Elston, Catherine. **Wolf Song: A Natural and Fabulous History of
    Wolves.** Jeremy P. Tarcher / Penguin. New York. 2004.

Sconduto, Leslie A. **Metamorphoses of the Werewolf: A Literary Study
    from Antiquity through the Renaissance.** McFarland & Company,
    Jefferson, North Carolina and London. 2008.

www.ingramcontent.com/pod-product-compliance
Lightning Source LLC
Chambersburg PA
CBHW021545290526
45785CB00004BA/1524